THE ILLUSTRATED
HISTORY OF
MOTORCYCLES

THE ILLUSTRATED HISTORY OF
MOTORCYCLES

Erwin Tragatsch

Quantum
Books

A QUANTUM BOOK

This book is produced by
Quantum Publishing Ltd.
6 Blundell Street
London N7 9BH

Copyright ©MCMLXXX
Quintet Publishing Limited.

This edition printed 2004

ISBN 1-86160-868-3

QUMIHOM

Phototypeset in England by Filmtype Services
Limited, Scarborough
Colour Separation by Sakai Lithocolour
Company Limited, Hong Kong
Printed in Singapore by
Star Standard Industries Pte Ltd

CONTENTS

INTRODUCTION

The author, on a 498cc four-cylinder Gilera works racing machine.

THIS ENCYCLOPEDIA lists in alphabetical sequence more than 2,500 makes of motorcycle, produced in at least 30 countries, from 1894 to the present day. The companies' commercial and sporting histories and their ranges of models, whether great or small, are discussed. Facts, figures, dates and technical details are provided. Many of the entries are illustrated, sometimes with hitherto-unpublished photographs.

Some of the early firms listed were very small, and assembled their machines entirely from bought-in parts, but all of them made production motorcycles. Companies which produced only 'one-offs', or which were merely workshops or dealers, are not included. The principal engines used by each manufacturer are detailed, and there are additional lists of important proprietary engines. There are also separate lists showing the major models of motorcycle produced throughout the world during interesting periods in the history of the industry.

I believe this to be the most comprehensive book of its kind, and I hope that it will be interesting not only to the motorcycle technician, dealer and sportsman but also to the collector, owner (past or present) or simply the enthusiast. When I began to compile my previous book *The World's Motorcycles, 1894–1963*, some of my friends in the industry suggested that I had engaged myself in an impossible task. When the book was published, it became a best-seller, filling a gap in the bookshelves of many a motorcycle enthusiast. That success led to the compilation of a much bigger book, with its extensive illustration.

This latest edition has been completely updated, new photographs have been included and some existing ones superseded by better illustrations.

My involvement with motorcycles has been lifelong. I have worked within the industry itself, in the motorcycle trade, in motor-sport, and in the motoring Press. My own experience, and widespread international research over a long period, have helped me fill the pages which follow. I have been helped by veteran riders, designers, manufacturers and their employees, many of them personal friends. Some of them have provided from memory details of machines which were built many decades ago.

Acquaintanceships have been renewed, and pleasant times recalled. It may have been 'impossible', but it was thoroughly enjoyable. I hope you enjoy it, too.

Erwin Tragatsch

8

THE PIONEER YEARS

IN THE SECOND half of the 19th century, both in Europe and in the USA, there were a good many attempts to build a practical steam bicycle. None was truly successful. Reducing engine and steam system to a manageable size and weight almost inevitably compromised power output and reliability, but the real drawback was the speed with which any steam engine evaporated its water. Topping-up the boiler feed water tank every ten or 15 miles was hardly convenient, or indeed always possible, while carrying a reserve supply was no answer at all. Few people did more to further the cause of the light steam-powered vehicle than the famous Count de Dion, yet his first sight of a very early petrol-engined car was enough to convince him that here lay the future. For all his success hitherto with steam, it was to the internal combustion engine that he immediately turned.

The internal combustion engine itself went through a considerable period of development and refinement. The earliest gas engines had no compression stroke and so were extremely inefficient. Etienne Lenoir's commercially successful workshop engine of 1860 drew in gas and air for half of one stroke, whereupon it was ignited, the subsequent expansion providing what power there was. Exhaust took place on the return stroke. The engine was 'double acting' — ignition took place on both sides of the piston. The four-stroke cycle of induction, compression, expansion and exhaust, proposed by French railway engineer Alphonse Beau de Rochas in 1862, was first attempted — and patented — by Nikolaus Otto of the Deutz gas engine works in Germany in 1876. Nine years later,

Otto's one-time colleagues, Gottlieb Daimler and Paul Maybach, tested a liquid-fuelled four stroke engine in a two wheeled chassis they called the 'Einspur'. Often spoken of as the world's first motorcycle, the Einspur, of course, was intended to test only the engine, but, in fact, it was a remarkably well thought-out and practical vehicle for its time.

Daimler's engine was astonishingly well adapted to automotive use. Light and self-contained, it was of 270cc, with the flywheel assembly enclosed in a cast aluminium crank-case, with a fan-cooled cast iron cylinder and cylinder head. The inlet valve opened automatically, while the exhaust valve was push-rod operated from a camtrack in the face of one of the flywheels. The 'benzene' (petrol) fuel was vaporised by passing air over its surface in a carburettor. Mistrusting electrical ignition, the inventors used a 'hot tube' of platinum, heated externally by a petrol-fuelled burner. The engine ran at the then remarkable speed of 800rpm, and produced something like half a horsepower.

That Europe was indeed ready for the automotive engine in 1885 is shown by the almost simultaneous appearance of petrol engined tricars from Karl Benz in Germany and Edward Butler in England. Of the two, Butler's was in its later, developed form far the more sophisticated, but repressive British traffic laws, not repealed until 1896, prevented it ever reaching commercial production. Butler's engine was fitted with rotary valves, a sort of primitive 'magneto' (actually dependent on the generation of static electricity rather than magnetic flux) and a spray carburettor, rather than a surface vaporiser.

Butler's patent on the carburettor prevented later inventors from obtaining a monopoly.

Count Albert De Dion and his partner Georges Bouton of the firm of De Dion, Bouton, probably did as much — and more — than anyone else to further the cause of the early motorcycle. They themselves concentrated in the 1890s on petrol-engined tricycles rather than on two wheelers, but their single-cylinder engine was suitable for both. In 1897 De Dion, Bouton offered these engines for sale to all comers, thus enabling scores of experimenters to copy — and improve upon — the remarkably successful machine popularised by the Werner brothers. As a result, the De Dion engine was copied — with and without acknowledgement — and made under licence all over the world, In its early form, the De Dion was of 70mm × 70mm 270cc, which was very soon uprated to 86mm × 86mm 500cc. As an indication of the De Dion's outstanding penetration of the market, it was significant that these were the engine dimensions chosen by Britain's newly formed Auto Cycle Club in 1903, when it came to standardise capacity classes for competition.

The engine was entirely conventional with air cooling, automatic inlet valve, surface carburettor and battery and coil ignition. However, it set new standards in precision engineering and provided a bench mark for power and reliability by which all other contemporary engines were judged. Needless to say, it soon had many rivals, of which the Belgian Minerva and the French Clement were the most popular, while inventors were quick to improve on the basic concept. As early as

Germany's Hildebrand and Wolfmuller Motorrad (left, top), the world's first production motor cycle. By the 1920s, BMW was leading the German industry, with its methodical production approach (left, bottom).

Infinitely variable ratio belt drive as used by Rudge (left, bottom). The pulleys expanded and contracted in sympathy to keep the belt adjusted. The 550cc side-valve Triumph, in the three-speed Sturmey Archer countershaft gearbox, was introduced in 1915 (right, bottom).

1898 in Britain, Coventry's Percy Riley, later to become a famous car maker, built an engine with a mechanically operated inlet valve, and went on to develop (and patent) 'overlap' valve timing. There were spray carburettors in profusion, one of the best of which was the British Amac of 1903. The hated and unreliable battery and coil ignition system was gradually superseded by the magneto, perfected through the work of Frederick Simms in England and Robert Bosch in Stuttgart in collaboration, first as a low-tension system and, then in 1902 as a high-tension one with rotating armature. (As a result of Bosch's developments, high tension magnetos became a virtual German monopoly, which led to some practical difficulties on the outbreak of the First World War in 1914).

Early development of the motorcycle seemed best advanced when it was left to the instincts of 'practical men' — gifted amateurs and superior blacksmiths, rather than formal engineers. This is no doubt a gross oversimplification, but certainly the purpose-designed Hildebrand and Wolfmuller Motorrad of 1894 was a failure, as was the equally impressive four-cylinder motor cycle designed by Colonel Holden — later to design the Brooklands track — a few years later. Both employed direct drive via the exposed connecting rods to crank axles on the rear spindle, which naturally severely limited engine speed and flywheel effect. In point of fact, the Motorrad had a capacity of no less than 1490cc, and made about 2hp at 380 rpm — at which engine speed of about 25mph was attained. All that bulk, weight and complication produced a performance that was put to shame by the Werner brothers' crude Motocyclette.

From time to time, other engineers took a look at the motorcycle of their day and decided that they could do better. In 1908, for instance T W Badgery of the James Cycle Co commissioned a design from the well thought of consulting engineer P L Renouf, which was the sensation of that year's London Motor Cycle Show. The 'Safety James' had a tubular chassis on car lines, centre-hub steering, quickly detachable wheels on single sided stub axles, and internal expanding brakes fore and aft. It had a 500cc single cylinder SV engine of James' own make, and belt drive, with an engine-pulley clutch. Alas, it was a monumental flop, and the James company rapidly turned to more orthodox designs. The response to the four-cylinder air-cooled 680cc Wilkinson TAC and later 850cc water-cooled TMC models was also disappointing. For 1910 and 1912, these offered truly advanced and luxurious specifications, but failed to sell in realistic numbers.

It seemed as though motor cycle design had to advance a bit at a time, not too precipitately and never too boldly. To be sure, Alfred Scott's radical two stroke twin of 1909 (1908 if you count six prototypes built by Jowett Brothers for development) found a market — but never a large one, even after Scott's TT wins in 1912 and 1913. And, in retrospect, the wonder is that the Scott sold at all, for not only was the two-stroke engine virtually unheard of, but this one was a twin and was partly — very soon fully — watercooled. The straight-tube triangulated frame, and the cylindrical fuel tank embracing the saddle tube must also have looked very strange to the average motor cyclist of 1909.

One of the Scott's most striking features was that it had a kickstarter — the first ever offered — and so the engine could be started at rest, and the machine moved off by engaging the lower of two 'gears' — actually two separate primary chains driving two sprockets on a countershaft with expanding clutches. The kickstart apart, there was nothing new about this. P & M, for one, had long since offered such a gear, as had many of the large V twin 'tricars' that were popular between about 1904 and 1909. What riders were demanding at about the same time as the Scott made its appearance, was a 'free engine' or clutch, and it was a big selling point for Triumph when they fitted a multi-plate clutch in the rear hub in 1909. There were, of course, even then, numerous proprietary clutches, usually incorporated in a special belt pulley.

Sprung front forks started to become really popular in about 1907. Again, many were proprietary fittings designed for use on older machines, though, for example, Quadrant had had such a front fork since 1903, while Rex had fitted them as standard since 1906.

Some of the early designs look downright dangerous to modern eyes, and probably were! Once again, the Scott of 1909 had perhaps the best design of all, with a true telescopic action. The famous Druid front fork, with parallel lever action controlled by coil springs first appeared in 1906, and became very popular — almost standard wear on British bikes and in successively modified form setting a fashion that was to last for 30 odd years and more.

Spring frames were the subject of many an invention in the early years, though very few of them had much merit. Curiously, those that enjoyed a certain success, such as the BAT, the Zenette and the much later Edmund, were not really spring frames at all, but sprung subframes, whereby the saddle and footrests were isolated together from road shocks. Such systems did absolutely nothing to help to

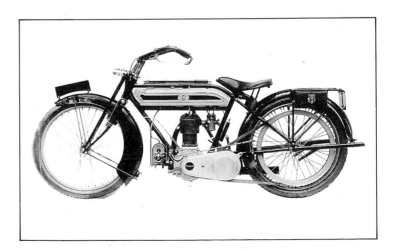

keep the rear wheel in contact with the road.

Lighting remained an afterthought. Few people rode at night in any case, and very few motor cycles were sold with lights of any sort. At first, cycle oil lamps were used, and sturdier versions were soon made. But from an early date, acetylene gas lighting became available and was soon accepted as standard. It might be messy and demand considerable looking after, but it was comparatively reliable and cheap.

As for brakes, the less said the better! Even so meticulous an engineer as Alfred Scott could at that time see no further than a cycle type stirrup at the front, and a shoe bearing on the inside of a drum formed in the rear chain sprocket. Front brakes were in any case regarded as mere 'bobby dodgers' not to be used — in the first place because they damaged the paint and plating of the front rim, but also because of the firm conviction that front brakes were dangerous. This superstition was a long time a-dying. As late as the 1960s a national survey in Britain found that over 40% of motor cyclists never used the front brake!

Change speed gears were a fruitful field for inventors in those early years. The 'adjustable pulley' was an early development, usually sold as a proprietary item and a not terribly satisfactory one at that. Early competition riders would carry two belts — one for use on the level, with the pulley flanges screwed close together to give a high ratio. When a freak hill had to be climbed, the pulley flanges were screwed apart and a slightly shorter belt fitted. The once famous Zenith Gradua and Rudge Multi systems were extensions of this idea. These took mechanical control of the driving pulley and, in the case of Zenith, actually automatically extended, or shortened, the wheelbase of the motor cycle to keep the belt taut. The Rudge Multi's rear pully flanges moved in and out in reverse sympathy with those on the engine pulley.

Quite a few simple two speed epicyclic gears — notably the NSU — made an early appearance, and eventually migrated to the rear hub in bicycle fashion. Such three-speed Armstong hubs featured strongly in the results of the 1911 Junior TT, held for the first time on the Mountain circuit in the Isle of

Early days in France and Germany. Above left: The first Daimler and Maybach two-wheeler. Left: The De Dion-Bouton three-wheeler. Above: Road conditions contrasted infavourably with those of the track. Right: Tessler tweaks a speed record on a British BAT in 1903.

THOSE MAGNIFICENT MEN ON THEIR CYCLING MACHINES

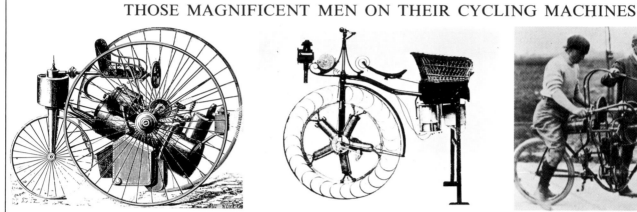

A steam engine, fired by petrol, powered this von Sauerbronn-Davis velocipede, 1883

The 1887 Millet prototype had a radial engine similar to those later used in aircraft

Propellor power . . . a chitty, chitty, bang bike by Anzani had its test flight in 1906

Look, no pedals! An ordinary bicycle gets a shove from an auxiliary engine . . . Italy, 1893

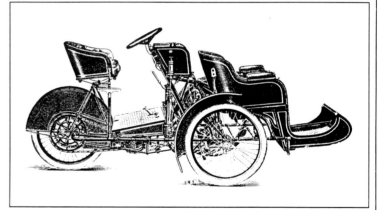

'Luxurious, high-powered, all-weather car-ette' . . . twin engined Quadrant, made in Britain, 1905

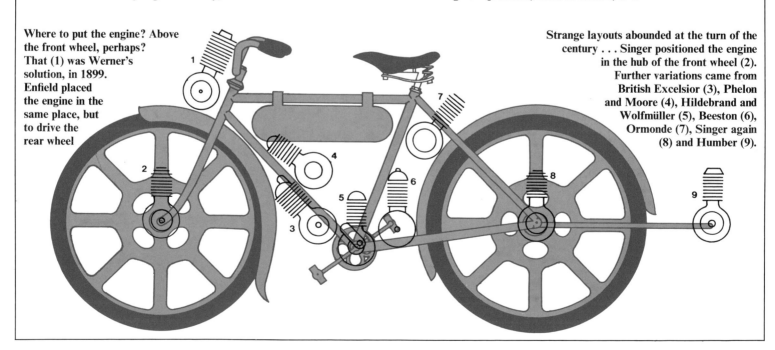

Where to put the engine? Above the front wheel, perhaps? That (1) was Werner's solution, in 1899. Enfield placed the engine in the same place, but to drive the rear wheel

Strange layouts abounded at the turn of the century . . . Singer positioned the engine in the hub of the front wheel (2). Further variations came from British Excelsior (3), Phelon and Moore (4), Hildebrand and Wolfmüller (5), Beeston (6), Ormonde (7), Singer again (8) and Humber (9).

In Czechoslovakia, Laurin & Klement produced the elegant single-cylinder B–D in 1903 (top), and more sporting versions such as the V-twin CCR (below). Bottom: Ludwig Opel with a 2¾ hp Opel motorcycle on army manoeuvres in 1905.

An early Scott two-stroke with water-cooled cylinder heads and air-cooled cylinders, telescopic front forks and all-chain drive (below) Acetylene powered this early headlamp (bottom).

Man. But the Indians that finished 1-2-3 in the Senior race that year, used countershaft gearboxes, and these made a big impression. Development of such gearboxes was rapid, and their wide acceptance really dated from the use by the Triumph company of the superb Sturmey Archer gearbox and clutch in their late Veteran masterpiece, the 550cc model H of despatch rider fame in the war years between 1914 and 1918.

Throughout the era, the side-valve engine reigned supreme. The ohv layout occasionally appeared for racing, but showed no great superiority. The theoretical advantages of overhead valves were, with compression ratios of about 4-1, more apparent than real, and valve steels being what they then were, the ohv layout was widely mistrusted for its threat of mechanical carnage from a 'dropped' valve. Pistons were universally of cast iron, though racing pistons were painstakingly (and expensively) machined from steel.

Ball and roller bearings were coming into use, especially for racing, but phosphor bronze bushes were still widely used, almost always lubricated by 'spit and hope' total loss systems. These depended upon a simple hand-operated pump transferring oil into the crankcase, whence it was distributed by 'splash'.

Two major companies — JAP, founded in 1903 and Precision dominated the engine scene, as far as Britain was concerned. Though the latter did not start making engines until 1910, their wares rapidly gained a fine reputation. The Stevens brothers of Wolverhampton had made engines of various sizes before settling for making the 350cc AJS motor cycle, while Dalton & Wade, Blumfeld and half a dozen others, long forgotten, also competed for a place. Of imported engines, the MAG, made by Motosacoche of Geneva, was by far and away the most successful.

Nor were these engines the 'longstrokes' beloved of ill-informed myth, but were mostly near-square in their bore and stroke configuration. Towards the end of the period, small capacity V twins became popular, and did well in competitions.

The 'Lightweight' — 250cc — class was hardly established before 1914. By that year, the weak and feeble machines, virtually motorised bicycles, that had struggled for a foothold in 1900, had become sturdy, powerful and reliable motorcycles that had, in the words of a contemporary writer, 'attained a state very close to perfection'. Such complacency invites mockery, but there is no doubt

that, looking back a mere 14 or 15 years, there was some excuse for it. The motor cycle, indeed, had come a long, long way. Few people realised how much further it still had to travel on the road to 'perfection'.

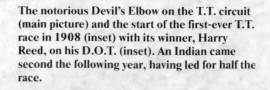

The notorious Devil's Elbow on the T.T. circuit (main picture) and the start of the first-ever T.T. race in 1908 (inset) with its winner, Harry Reed, on his D.O.T. (inset). An Indian came second the following year, having led for half the race.

THE AMERICAN STORY

A STEAM-POWERED bicycle built by Sylvanus Roper in 1870 is still preserved in the Smithsonian Museum in Washington DC, the real involvement of the USA in the story of the motorcycle dates from the importation of a De Dion tricycle in 1898 by Hiram Maxim who, at the time, was — among his many other activities — consulting engineer to Colonel A A Pope's Columbia bicycle manufacturing concern. Columbia, in fact, were the first company to offer a motorcycle for sale in the country in 1900; within months, they had a dozen competitors, none of whom offered much more than the crudest of specifications.

In early 1901, however, the Indian, designed by Springfield bicycle maker, George M Hendee, and toolmaker Oscar Hedstrom, made its first appearance. Its strengthened bicycle frame, retaining the pedalling gear, incorporated the single cylinder engine as part of the seat tube, and thus inclined rearwards. It had an automatic inlet valve and an ingenious spray carburettor of Hedstrom's own design, but the engine itself, though designed by Hedstrom was made by the Thor Manufacturing Co, as were all Indian engines until 1905.

From the start, Indian used chain drive to the rear wheel as did most of their rivals. Curiously, one of the few makes to use belt drive — and to persist with it until 1912 — was the Harley Davidson, first produced for sale in 1904. Though Indian sales were modest at first — 143 machines in 1902 — success came quickly, after good showings in early endurance events, and Hendee and Hedstrom

pursued a policy of innovation and improvement. In 1907, when sales were in the thousands, a V twin engine of 600cc was introduced, built by Indian themselves, with the 'Hedstrom motor' cast into the crankcase. One such machine, with twistgrip throttle control and a sprung front fork, was shipped to Britain, where it took part in the ACC's 1000-mile trial, winning a gold medal. Indian were already extremely alive to the possibilities of export to Europe, and especially to Britain.

In 1909, expatriate American W H Wells was made British concessionaire, and entered himself and George Lee Evans in the Senior TT in the Isle of Man. Sensationally, Evans led the race for half its distance, finishing a close second to Matchless rider Harry Collier. In 1910, Indian introduced a two-speed countershaft gearbox and clutch. Already successful at home in pure speed events on board tracks, they now provided Wells' English agency with racing machines that competed with spectacular success at Brooklands. And for the 1911 Senior TT, run for the first time on the famous Mountain circuit, Indian visited in force, with George Hendee himself, Oscar Hedstrom, ace rider Jake de Rosier, and a full compliment of machinery and race mechanics. They meant to win — and win they did, with their British riders taking the first three places. In 1912, Indian's sales reached 20,000.

Not that Indian had it entirely their own way in America in the first decade of the new century. In racing, and especially in board track

ley Davidson favoured belt drive (bottom right), but of their competitors followed.

One of the all-conquering Indians in the 1911 Senior T.T., seen here at Union Mills. The rider, C.B. Franklyn, was later a leading designer for Springfield.

racing, they had serious rivals in Excelsior, Merkel and Cyclone. Harley Davidson, who made their first V twin in 1909, did not race themselves, but were happy to advertise the success of private owners. And by about 1912, there were at least 30 well-established makes that almost had the status of household names, in US motorcycle manufacturing.

By that time a pattern had been established. Roads that were atrocious by European standards demanded sturdier frames. Front forks were usually of the bottom link pattern and again very robust. Twist grips were common for controls, with the throttle usually on the left, and piano wires were used rather than the Bowden cable that was ubiquitous in Europe.

Brakes were, if anything, ahead of those in Europe, a popular system being a contracting band and expanding shoes using the same drum on the rear wheel. Similarly, American carburettors, such as the Holley, Schebler and Hedstrom, were definitely ahead of their European counterparts. Much attention was paid to comfort, with large and elaborately suspended saddles and sturdy metal footboards. Spring frames were not common, but when offered, as by Pope, they were of sound design. Europeans found American controls difficult. As noted above, the throttle was usually controlled by the left hand, but so were the gears if any and, often, even the clutch — this might have a lever alongside the left hand side of the tank as well as a foot pedal, also on the left.

Lighting and electrical equipment was generally excellent. The US manufacturers did not make the mistake of depending on Germany for magnetos, and offered electric lighting as standard, long before it was thought of in Europe. Indian, indeed, scored a notable 'first' in 1914 with the all electric 'Hendee special' featuring electric starting! Though this innovation was a failure, costing the company a good deal of money, it illustrates Indian's forward-looking attitude.

As early as 1914, however, economic forces were at work that could not be denied. Quite a few of the pioneer names had already disappeared in the face of determined marketing by Indian, Harley Davidson and Excelsior. Now the appearance of incredibly cheap cars, such as Ford's Model T, was to eat into the sales of motorcycles, so it was no coincidence that, between 1915 and 1918, such well thought of companies as Pope, Yale, Iver Johnson, Cyclone, Thor and Peerless ceased production along with many others. Of those 'household names' a mere half dozen survived into the 1920s and only Indian, Harley Davidson and Excelsior lasted out the decade.

Excelsior — sold in Europe as 'the American X' — had sprung from Ignatz Schwin's bicycle manufacturing company in Chicago in 1908 and during the war years had absorbed the Detroit-built four-cylinder in-line Henderson, which Excelsior were to sell in vastly improved form post-war. In-line fours, indeed, became something of a cult in the USA. They had their origin in the Pierce Arrow of 1909, a free-hand copy of an imported Belgian FN. The Pierce lasted just long enough to inspire the Henderson, first made in 1912. Post war, the Henderson brothers left Excelsior to make the Ace, which, when Bill Henderson was killed in a road accident, passed in due course to Indian. As the Indian Four, it remained in production until the USA entered the Second World War in 1941.

The USA's other highly respected in-line four was the Cleveland, made from 1925 to 1929. All of these were extremely powerful luxurious motorcycles with tireless performance. As much as anything, they exemplified a general US trend in the 1920s towards a super sporting performance that no car — cheap or otherwise — could provide. With a power-to-weight ratio at least three times better than that of a powerful car, US V twins and fours were used in large numbers by the police, the armed forces and, to a lesser extent, by public utilities. They also sold to sporting enthusiasts, the V twins forming the backbone of

Class C Amateur racing in the 1930s. The demands of off-road competition, hill climbing, and long distances on the vastly improved roads of that era resulted in motorcycles that, to European eyes, soon became grotesquely over-engineered.

Excelsior had dropped out of contention in 1931 to concentrate on bicycles and, for most of the 1930s, Indian and Harley Davidson were on a fairly equal footing in almost every respect. There was one vital difference, however. George Hendee had retired from his Indian company in 1916. Harley Davidson remained firmly in the hands of the families who had started it back in the pioneer days of the 1900s.

The 1930s saw a general stagnation in design, confirmed rather than otherwise by Class C competition, which limited amateur racing to side-valve engines of 750cc. An afterthought in the regulations allowed over-head-valve engines of 500cc, though this remained academic, until Canadian rider Billy Matthews won the 1941 Daytona 200 mile race on a Norton International! The overwhelming popularity of British motor cycles in the USA after the Second World War was a phenomenon that the local industry could never have foreseen. Harley Davidson retrenched — and bought out the Italian Aermacchi company between 1956 and 1960. Indian, however, tried to meet the invasion head on with a totally new European-type range, the so-called 'Torque' models, the 220cc (later 250cc) and 440cc (later 500cc) single-cylinder Arrow and vertical twin Scout. A 1000cc in-line four was also planned. At this point, the British company J Brockhouse & Co provided a massive capital injection that gave them control, not only of the Indian Sales Corporation, but of manufacturing at Springfield. Losses on the

During the First World War, the American Forces ordered 70,000 Harleys, some rigged as armed outfits (above). Britain had a Clyno-Vickers machine-gun outfit (below).

The first Yank and Harley to enter Germany 11/12/18

Torque range forced Brockhouse to suspend manufacture in 1953 and subsequent 'Indians' sold in America were thinly-disguised British models. Indian's long and honourable history was over.

Harley Davidson took a different view of the US market. Arguing that, though lightweights might be popular, there would always be sales for the traditionally rugged style of native motorcycle, they re-designed and updated their big V twins and elevated their ownership into a cult. They were able to use their Italian connection to satisfy the consid-

Historic border-crossing (left) by Harley-Davidson on Armistice Day, 1918. British dispatch-riders used machines by Phelan and Moore, Douglas, BSA, Triumph and others.

erable demand for cheaper and lighter models with at least an American name, meanwhile doggedly improving their bigger and better V twins. The Aermacchi connection was severed in the late 1970s. By that time, persistance, determination and excellence of management had once again made Harley Davidson a force to be reckoned with in the US market. They had survived the British invasion, the subsequent flooding of the market by the Japanese and the brief era of Spanish imports. In the 1980s, indeed, Japanese manufacturers paid Harley Davidson the ultimate compliment of blatantly copying their layout and styling! Harley Davidson's survival — and survival in good health and on their own terms — is one of the most fascinating episodes in motor cycling's long and honourable history.

Small-town America, 1910. A Sunday morning gathering of enthusiasts in Nebraska, about to set off for a 150-mile jaunt.

The mid-1930s Harley Davidson (left) and Indian (right), both the product of Class C amateur racing.

THE 1920s...THE GOLDEN AGE

GOLDEN AGES BECOME so only in retrospect, so no doubt motor cyclists everywhere grumbled just as much about their grievances in the years between the wars as they ever did before, or have done since. Those years, however, definitely saw enormous changes for the better, both in the economic circumstances of the average enthusiast — this was the first time ordinary wage earners found themselves able to afford to buy and run a motor cycle — and in the way motor cycles were designed.

If the average motor cycle of 1939 is compared with that of 1919, the average enthusiast would marvel not so much at the differences but at the improvements. Side valves have given way to overhead versions, which are fully enclosed at that, quietened by a copious circulation of oil that, as a bonus, carries away excessive heat from the cylinder head. The lubrication system itself is vastly improved, with, instead of the arbitrary injection of oil by a simple hand-operated pump, automatic engine-driven pumps circulating it to every vital part and allowing it to cool by returning it to the oil tank. Dubious three-speed gearboxes with clumsy hand change have given way to foolproof four-speed varieties, operated by a foot pedal. Brakes have improved beyond belief. So have tyres, which are now wired onto the rims rather than held on by air pressure. No longer does a deflated tyre roll off the rim in lethal fashion. Transmission belts have been replaced by chains. Even the cheapest lightweight two-stroke has electric lighting, usually with a battery and automatic control that ensures correct charging by the built-in dynamo.

The motor cycle of 1939, therefore, is altogether a more practical affair than its 1919 ancestor. It is easier to clean, too, with lavish user of untarnishable, durable chromium plating in place of nickel, which, unless laboriously polished, dulled to a dirty grey within weeks. Performance has been transformed as well. Between the first post-war Senior TT of 1920 and that of 1939, the speed had risen from the 51.48mph of Tommy de la Hay's side-valve Sunbeam to the staggering 89.38mph of Georg Meier's supercharged double ohc BMW twin.

Such was the universal appeal of motor cycling in these years that, despite local influences and accidents that shaped the designs of one national industry along other lines to those of another, progress was constant, in Europe at any rate. That the same was not true of the USA was not the fault of the US motor-cycle industry.

In fact, the best American motor cycles of 1919 were considerably in advance of most of their European contemporaries. Pre war, the US industry had already standardised the use of countershaft gearboxes, while, in Europe flimsy epicyclic hub gears had been all the rage. Similarly, the USA had gone over to chain drive, while Europe stuck to the belt. The motor cycles themselves were handsome, powerful and robustly made. The factories were superbly equipped, taking advantage of the most up-to-date production methods, which meant that US machines could be shipped across the Atlantic and still sell at competitive prices. They did so in sufficient quantities to panic the British and European domestic industries into demanding that tariff barriers should be erected to half this penetration. This came to pass. For all their vision and efficiency, US manufacturers were abruptly denied access to an export market that had become vital to them, because cheap cars, a menace before the war, now threatened the very existence of the domestic American motor cycle.

The industry shrank and retrenched, with many of the companies that had survived until now disappearing. The 'big three' — Indian, Harley Davidson and Excelsior (makers of big V twins as well as the superb Henderson four) — were forced to depend on what export markets were left to them, and on sales to the police, the armed forces, pubic utilities, and sportsmen. Excelsior stopped manufacture in the face of the depression in 1931, leaving Indian and Harley Davidson to fight out their bitter rivalry.

The USA's vanishing motor cycle industry was saved in the 1930s by the introduction of Class C Amateur racing, whose regulations specified little more than basically standard production machines with 750cc side-valve engines should be used. Events comprised a strange mix of road racing, enduro runs, TT racing, flat track and speedway contents. TT racing was on a dirt surface, with gradients and left and right turns. Flat track was on loose-surfaced tracks of up to half a mile, while speedway racing took place on longer tracks with steeply banked turns.

Class C was an instant success. After 1937, when Daytona Beach became its focal point, a genuine revival of interest in motor cycles and motorcycling resulted. On the other hand, however, the somewhat restrictive formula and the need for one motor cycle to fulfill so many functions led to stagnation and moved the US motor cycle far away from the concepts of European design.

There was another facet of the US scene, particularly in urban California, that is often forgotten. This was the motor scooter, which cropped up over and over again in the years between the wars. It was one such scooter, an American Autoped, owned by a prominent English member of parliament, that found its way into an article in early 1919 in the *Daily News* and started a craze in Britain that amounted to a mania. The newspaper was swamped with letters, literally by the sackful. A rumour that one London store had Autopeds in stock saw people queuing half way down Oxford Street. The interest spilled over into the motor cycle magazines though, to give them their due, the editorial staff showed little enthusiasm. Every week saw dozens of projected designs, most of them crude and impractical. Many small under-capitalised firms were set up to build scooters and a few actually staggered into production, by which time the mania had subsided. This left concerns such as ABC Skootamota, Kenilworth and Autoglider — high and dry. No wonder that British manufacturers hesitated when Italian and German scooters appeared on the market 30 odd years later.

Curiously, though the craze for scooters did not reach the same height in Germany, it

The post-war years saw a short-lived craze for the scooter (left). The unorthodox 5-cylinder Megola was raced by Toni Bauhofer and reached speeds up to 140 km/h.

lasted longer, and DKW made scooters that at least sold in reasonable numbers. Expatriate Danish engineer J S Rasmussen had founded his DKW company at Zschopan near Chemnitz in Saxony to build steam lorries — Dampe Kraft Wagen — but quickly switched after 1919 to making clip-on auxiliary engines for bicycles, scooters and ultra lightweight motor cycles, all powered by simple two-stroke engines designed by Herman Weber. These engines were also widely sold in Germany to other makers. Though DKW did make larger

machines, favourable tax concessions meant that the vast majority were of 200cc and less.

Somehow, the company managed to survive the appalling hyper-inflation of 1923 that killed off so many other concerns and indeed flourished mightily. They began racing in the 175cc and later 250cc classes with Hugo Ruppe-designed engines, utilising his patented Ladepumpe charging piston below the crankcase. Soon these 'blown' DKWs demanded water cooling to cope with their power. They were extremely successful

in road racing and in the long-distance hill climbs so popular in Germany. However, in Grand Prix racing they were not really a match for the British four-strokes, or, for that matter, the Austrian Puchs, which used a split-single two-stroke engine, also pump-charged.

So soundly were DKW beaten by Puch in the 1930 and 1931 seasons that they called in designer Arnold Zoller, who laid out split-single racing engines — still using the charging piston — that were gradually developed into

'Lawrence of Arabia' (big picture) owned no less than eight Brough-Superior machines. In the bottom picture, from the left, designer and manufacturer George Brough, racer Eddy Meyer and works manager Ike Webb outside the factory in 1927.

the most powerful two-strokes that the world had ever seen. As a result, DKW won the 250cc European championship in 1934, 1935 and 1938 and both the 250cc and 350cc championships in 1939. Perhaps their finest achievement was Ewald Kluge's 1938 Lightweight TT win at over 80mph, a result that convinced even the most sceptical.

Germany's other most celebrated and successful motor cycle between the wars was the BMW, first seen at the Paris Salon of 1923. Originally war-time aircraft engine makers, BMW had embarked on a number of enterprises before starting to manufacture a proprietary flat-twin motor cycle engine. They then decided to make a motor cycle of their own, with shaft drive, so that a transverse engine layout and unit gearbox were natural features to incorporate. Like DKW, BMW raced from an early date with great success and adopted supercharging wholeheartedly. Rider Ernst Herne held the world's fastest record no less than six times in the 1930s, BMW won the 500cc European championship of 1938, and in 1939, riders Georg Meier and Jock West finished first and second in the Senior TT.

Innovative and superbly crafted, the big BMW bikes were very expensive as befitted what were probably the best motor cycles in the world in those years. They did make smaller, somewhat less expensive single-cylinder models of between 200cc and 400cc — still with shaft drive — but exclusivity was BMW's trademark. Next to Britain's, the German industry between the wars was probably the busiest in Europe, despite economically troubled times. Strangely, many firms, by no means obscure concerns, used British engines, gearboxes and other proprietary components. To some extent, this was a tribute to the efficiency of the British industry and its resulting low prices, but it also reflected the esteem in which British motor cycles were held on the continent. JAP, Blackburne, Sturmey Archer (Raleigh) and Python (Rudge) engines were widely used, as were the Bradshaw oil-cooled engine and the remarkable Barr & Stroud sleeve valve. It was a considerable loss to Britain when Adolf Hitler came to power and put an end to this widespread dependence on imported compoents. No less was it a source of embarrassment to those German firms left high and dry.

As in Germany, France saw an upsurge of interest in motor cycling immediately after the First World War and a number of imaginative and advanced designs were produced.

Aircraft makers Bleriot and engine manufacturers Gnome et Rhone both saw the mass production of motor cycles as the solution for factories suddenly made idle. The former showed interesting vertical twins, while the latter chose to build the British ABC under licence. Somehow, however, French enthusiasm was short-lived, though the native industry tried hard to keep up with the latest technological developments, this soon became little more than a prestige exercise at the annual Paris Salon. What did sell, and in numbers that kept the industry alive if not exactly flourishing, was the 100cc Velomo-

teur that was untaxed and could be ridden without even the formality of a driving licence.

Nor was there the sporting interest in France that so sustained motor cycling in Germany. The French Grand Prix turned into an ill-supported and even worse attended farce. The magnificent racing complex built at Montlhery, 20 miles from Paris, never paid its way — though the 1.7-mile banked track was popular for record breaking. Yet, strangely, the 'speed week' at Arpajon, held on a narrow tree-lined stretch of road with a four mile undulating straight, attracted entrants from all over Europe, while the Bol d'Or, an extraordinary 24-hour race with no change of rider, that started in 1924 on a public road circuit in the forest of St Germain near Paris, survived for the next 15 years. The first race was won by an 500cc ohv Sunbeam, victory in it remaining a British preserve, which makes its survival all the more surprising.

Italy was a late comer to motor cycle manufacture, but, as the 1920s wore on, made up for it in full measure. Garelli and Moto Guzzi joined Gilera and Frera as sporting makers, as did Benelli and Bianchi. Italian designers were early and enthusiastic advocates of ohv and ohc engines and the use of light alloy components and soon developed a sense of style that they have never lost.

Racing — especially long-distance open road racing from town to town — became an Italian institution. With the supercharged Rondine — later Gilera — the Italians could justly have claimed to have begun the trend to four-cylinder racing machines. Dorino Serafini's European title on the 500cc Gilera in 1939 was a taste of things to come. Moto Guzzi first raced in the TT in 1926, and in 1935 were rewarded when Stanley Woods won both Lightweight and Senior races. And in 1937 on a Moto Guzzi Omobono Tenni won the Lightweight TT — the first foreign rider ever to win a TT.

Yet, for all their excellence and sporting pedigree, Italian motor cycles were virtually unknown elsewhere in Europe. Given their reputation in racing and in the International Six Days Trial, why the Italians made no attempt to export is hard to understand. Perhaps it was because, as in Germany, taxation encouraged smaller engines, so many of those exquisite Italian ohc models were of 250cc and below.

Without doubt, however, it was the British industry that dominated European motor cycling between the wars. To some extent, this was because it enjoyed a virtually 'captive' colonial export market, particularly in Australia, but there was naturally more to it than that. The concentration of diverse skills and experience in the British Midlands, the intense competition between not only motor cycle manufacturers, but also the makers of proprietary equipment, and the part played by an unsensational and responsible specialist press all played their parts.

Though British design ws perhaps conservative, this may have been no bad thing — evolution is better than revolution, as history seems to show. In addition, many British designers were only too aware of the strange story of the post-war ABC. This wonder motor cycle, with its 400cc ohv flat twin engine set transversely across the frame, unit construction car-type gearbox with gate change by hand lever, self-dumping leaf-spring suspension fore and aft, internal expanding brakes, ingenious frame design and electric lighting with built-in dynamo, embodied everything that a motor cyclist could wish, including generous weather protection.

Designed by the young Granville Bradshaw, the ABC truly appeared to be ten — even 20 — years ahead of its time when it was revealed in prototype form early in 1919. The machine was to be made by the Sopwith aviation and engineering company in a purpose-equipped factory, with a production target of 10,000 a year, but despite the brilliance of the overall concept and Sopwith's money, the ABC was a damaging fiasco. It took 15 months to reach production, only for Sopwith to go into voluntary liquidation after fewer than 2,500 motor cycles had been made. A disappointed British public turned to the next best, which might not be all that much ahead of the times, but which did at least live up to its maker's claims and its reputation.

Such British marques as Sunbeam, Norton,

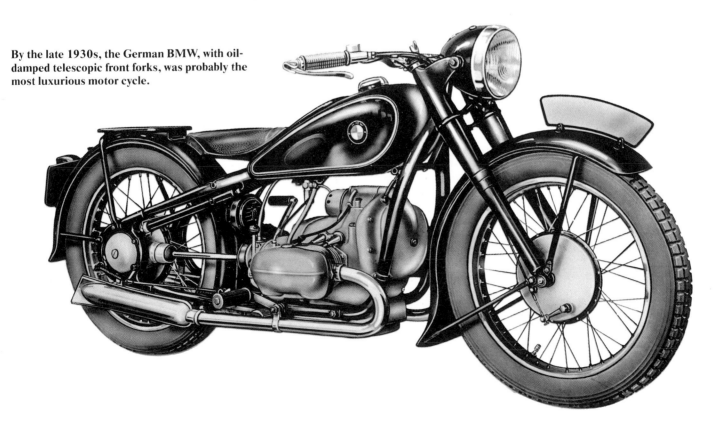

By the late 1930s, the German BMW, with oil-damped telescopic front forks, was probably the most luxurious motor cycle.

Shown here with his 996cc Zenith, designer and rider Bert le Vack broke many records. Bottom picture: Swiss MAG-engined German Standard machines in the 1928 ADAC five-country trial. The riders are (from left) Pail Rüttchen and Eugen Gerlach.

AJS, Scott, BSA and Triumph sold world wide. British bikes won the TT year after year and the European Grand Prix races as well. Britain's dominance of the market extended beyond the super-sports mould into other areas as well. There were plenty of companies using the 270cc Villiers two-stroke engine, or the small side-valve engines made by JAP or Blackburne. As in Germany, there were many 'manufacturers' who made little themselves, assembling their motor cycles almost entirely from bought-in components. This could be an expensive method, especially for the smaller firms who could not bargain quantity against prices, as could a larger company, such as, say, OK Supreme. Many small firms, and quite a few larger ones were under capitalised, and so did not survive the depression of the early 1930s. Some, however, flourished. New Imperial, for instance, began to make their own engines in the mid 1920s and went on to introduce their own range of unit construction engines and gearboxes and their own cantilever spring frames in the 1930s. Vincent HRD became their own engine makers in the 1930s, as did Excelsior with the famous Manxman ohc engines, which they took over when Blackburne stopped making motorcycle engines.

The king of the assemblers was the incomparable George Brough, who, working from his small Nottingham factory, advertised his Brough Superiors as 'The Rolls Royce of motor cycles'. Brough always insisted on the best, was his own head tester and rode his own machinery in trials and speed events with great success.

Brough Superiors really were hand-made. Having ordered one and paid a deposit, customers were encouraged to visit the factory several times to check on progress. On each visit they were expected to pay a further installment — a procedure that, on the one hand, mad the eventual settling of a the final bill less painful, and, on the other, gave Brough a healthy cash flow.

Most of Brough's machines used big V twin JAP (and in later years Matchless) engines, though he built several 'show stoppers' — a transverse engined V twin, a narrow angle V four and an in-line air-cooled four-in-line, it is doubtful if he had any serious intention of making any of them. However, he did make a dozen or so outfits with an 800cc water-cooled Austin 7 engine, gearbox and shaft drive, with the final drive unit between closely two-strokes — entered the market with a set twin rear wheels. Unfortunately, the outbreak of war in 1939, stopped the development of another model that Brough certainly intended to make. This was the ill-fated 1000cc transverse flat four Golden Dream, with contra-rotating crankshafts, unit gearbox and shaft drive. It had been the sensation of the 1938 Motor Cycle Show. If 1920s were the years of development, the 1930s were those of consolidation. The depression of the early 1930s that eliminated many small companies — and brought changes of ownership to several larger ones — only confirmed the conviction that sales depended upon value for money. The resilience of the motor cycle industry was quite remarkable. The years between the wars culminated with the birth of — not a new motor cycle, but a new style of motor cycle — Edward Turner's 500cc Triumph twin. Nothing new in itself, the Speed Twin and its super sports version, the Tiger 100, opened up a whole new prospect. To have been young, to have been able to buy and run a Triumph Twin in 1937 must have been exciting indeed! Little did those lucky few realise what lay ahead not so far in the future. But that is the way of the world, and we cannot blame those who experienced those days — and indeed those who only read about them — from regarding the years between the wars as a Golden Age.

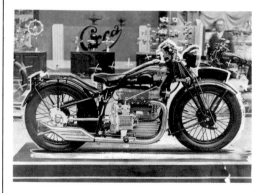

This superb 750cc four-cylinder Moto-became dates from the late 1930s; the average Frenchman in the inter-war years, however, was more likely to be riding the 100cc Velomoteur.

THE STORY OF AN INDUSTRY

THE HISTORY OF ANY long-lived enterprise is shaped by more forces than we usually believe, and the history of the motorcycle industry — and of motorcycles — is no exception.

Foremost — without which there would be no story — was the work of countless individuals. Many of them are now forgotten, though some are remembered, while a few have become legends, but all of them, in whichever country and at whatever time, had to contend with the changing world around them.

Advances in technology, improved materials, new inventions, all had to be taken on board. So did fluctuations in prosperity and the rise and fall of different markets. Changing prices of raw materials — and of petrol — were important. Taxes and tariffs — on imports or exports — could be altered at the stroke of a pen. And industrial strife and unrest could play a major part. These and a thousand other factors over a span of more than 90 years, explain many apparent anomalies.

Early improvements to motorcycles included spray carburettors and high tension magneto ignition, both of which improved reliability beyond belief. Throttle and ignition controls were moved from the tank top to the handlebars and operated by Bowden cables. Automatic inlet valves gave way to mechanical operation. By about 1907, spring front forks were becoming common. Engines were almost all of about 500cc with side valves; larger V twins of up to 1000cc were usually used when a sidecar was to be pulled.

There had been two speed transmissions from a very early date, notabl that designed by Richard Moore of P & M in 1904, but early engines were enormously flexible, and fixed ratio single speed transmission with V belt drive lasted a long time. A belt was light, cheap and gave wonderfully smooth drive without an expensive shock absorber or cush drive. While they might slip in wet weather, belts did not rapidly wear out, from the mud and grit thrown up from water-bound Macadam roads as did exposed chains. Various 'free engine' clutches and variable ratio pulleys were offered from an early date as proprietary fittings; the ingenious Zenith Gradua and Rudge Multi systems of 'infinitely variable' drive prolonged the life of belt drive up to and beyond the First World War.

Brakes in early days were crude. At the front, there was simply a cycle-type stirrup, which nobody used for fear of a front wheel skid on the loose surfaced roads. At the rear,

The scene outside the Rudge depot at the 1911 T.T. Victor Surridge (nearest camera) was killed during a crash in practice shortly after this — the first T.T. fatality.

there was a shoe that wedged into the belt drive rim. But except in cities, traffic was almost unbelievably sparse.

Such was the general state of the motorcycle in Britain and Europe in about 1907. In that year, there were two innovations that were to affect the British industry enormously and help to make it the strongest in Europe by 1914. the 2¾-mile banked track at Brooklands was opened. Subsequently, this was to prove a testing ground that played a valuable role for over 30 years until it was closed for ever by the outbreak of war in 1939. Of even more importance was the Tourist Trophy race in the Isle of Man. Racing in Europe had lost its way since open road events had been banned after the catastrophic Paris-Madrid race of 1903. The main European event, the International Cup, was an ill conceived farce that was not even spectacular, for only three entries were allowed from each country.

Nor did International Cup regulations do anything to spur development of real motorcycles, for engines of unlimited size were allowed with no fuel consumption limits, whilst at the same time, total weight had to be under 110 lb. Cheating, too, was endemic. British riders, disgusted by the 1906 fiasco, approached the Auto Cycle Club of Britian, and the result was the TT.

The Auto Cycle Union, as it had become by 1907, framed regulations year by year that really did 'improve the breed'. Run at first on the 14-odd mile St John course, the race proved a real test and speeds and reliability improved year by year.

The winning speed rose from 38mph in 1907 to over 50mph in 1910. The ACU then — to encourage development of change speed gears — moved the race to the 37½ mile Mountain circuit, which, slightly altered in 1920 to 37¾ miles and improved beyond belief over many years, is still in use today. European manufacturers took part from the start, while, by 1911, such was the TT's prestige that Indian came all the way from the USA to compete — and were rewarded by a 1-2-3 Senior win. This was a shock to British pride, but it was to be a further 24 years before there was another foreign victory.

The outbreak of war in 1914 had little influence on either the industry or on design, though the drying-up of German supplies meant that the making of magnetos had to developed. A few radical post-First World War designs, notably the transverse twin ABC, excited much interest, but the ABC died of slapdash hasty design and the ineptitude of its sponsors — the wartime airframe makers, Sopwith.

Countershaft gearboxes and chain drive — both pioneered by Indian (and made acceptable by their TT win) took over in the early 1920s and gearbox manufacture became another speciality.

Proprietary engine makers fought each

other to a standstill that soon left JAP and Blackburne the survivors with some opposition from the oil-cooled Bradshaw and the unique sleeve valve Barr & Stroud. 'Assembled' motor cycles flourished, their builders making nothing themselves, but buying in engines, frames, gearboxes, wheels, tanks, saddles and other components from the huge infrastructure that had developed. Villiers of Wolverhampton became suppliers of proprietary two-stroke engines to the world. Nor were British exports confined to its empire. Germany became so dependent upon the British industry that by 1930, purchases of engines, gearboxes and other components reached a value exceeded only by exports of complete motor cycles to Australia.

Italy too, was a good customer, for the Italian industry was a late starter. Sunbeam, Norton, AJS and other sporting British machines had a ready sale there. So, too, was France, where the native industry took an easy option, largely making a living from 'Velomoteurs' of 100cc that sold for not much more than the price of a bicycle and needed no road tax, licence or insurance.

Between the wars, the motorcycling world believed that British was best, even though good, even great motorcycles were being made elsewhere. Germany's BMW and DKW, Belgium's FN and Switzerland's Motosacoche, Italy's Gilera and Moto Guzzi, were all excellent makes as were many more. But between the wars, Britain undoubtedly led the world. America's early promise had faded with the success of Henry Ford's Model T. With the Tin Lizzie costing less than a good

motorcycle, only the market for heavy, large capacity high performances bikes was left, exemplified by Indian and Harley Davidson. As American design became introverted and the machines ever bigger and heavier, it lost its appeal in other markets.

After the Second World War, a policy of austerity and petrol rationing at home meant that the British bought mainly utility 125cc and 197cc two-strokes, but the industry set to with a will to sell, to America sporting 500cc and later 600cc and 650cc machines modelled on Triumph's successful pre-war Speed Twin. However, unknowingly, the British industry had entered an era of stagnation. For the moment, it was too easy. Even the dreary little two-strokes found export buyers in their tens of thousands, but, over the next dozen years or so, these markets, most of them in 'empire' countries, were to contract and disappear behind trade barriers favourable to them, but not to the British. Eventually, the only real overseas market left was the USA. The actual home market shrank too — far too much to support the whole industry. A second-hand car rather than a sidecar outfit became the working man's transport. With the appearance of the Austin Morris Mini, the ordinary motor cycle was doomed.

The British industry, with its eye on the USA, seemed particularly inept over the one area that was left in the home market. The appearance of 50cc mopeds from Germany and Italy produced no response. BSA had made a dreadful job of the clever, but flawed, BSA Dandy, while their 75cc Beagle and the 50cc Ariel Pixie scarecely saw production.

Thus, the Japanese — in particular Honda — from a vast and protected home market, were able to penetrate Britain at a level that the domestic manufacturers hardly acknowledged as existing.

When Honda launched their four cylinder 750cc CB750 in the USA in 1969, it gave the British a mortal blow. In an era of high taxation and dreadful labour relations, the BSA company made some terrible blunders and with the ill fated 350cc BSA Fury and Triumph Bandit twins, missed the market entirely for the 1972 season. The Japanese moved in for the kill, and the rest is history.

When the late Erwin Tragatsch first compiled this monumental work, he lamented the still recent facts. 'The saddest story of all', he called the death of the British industry with which he had been so well acquainted. He blamed bad management — of which in later years there had been more than enough. But he also blamed bad government — a point often overlooked by commentators with no experience of business. Yet could anything have saved British motor cycles? Probably not, in view of the shrinking home market, except protectionist policies which no British government would countenance. Germany's proud and confident industry largely collapsed in the late 1950s because of overproduction, rising domestic affluence, the

Inside the machine shop of an early motor cycle factory. Though the actual bikes have changed dramatically, manufacturing methods have not altered that substantially; contrast this picture of a modern Japanese plant with the previous one, which dates from the turn of the century.

The Honda CB750 four-cylinder 'superbike' (below) ended the dominance of large British machines in America. Bottom: Two motorcycling milestones — the 50cc NSU Quickly moped (left) and the tiny Honda 'stepthrough' (right) that emerged a decade later.

appearance of cheap cars and failure to export. Italy's industry was horribly weakened at the same time by labour troubles and, though the Italians did adopt a protectionist attitude, much of what is left of their industry has entered the 1990s in very indifferent health.

It is easy to forget that for roughly 25 years there was a flourishing Spanish industry with quite remarkable export sales to the USA. It was hampered — and yet at the same time protected — by the Franco regime's insistence on self sufficiency, and export successes were largely based on the low Spanish labour costs of the time. But when Spain again became part of the European community, its industry was as vulnerable as any to the Japanese.

Worldwide, sales of motor cycles have dropped to such a low total figure that the output of one vigorous and extremely efficient industry, the Japanese, can satisfy the entire demand. In fact it can more than satisfy it, and signs are that even the Japanese industry is suffering from over-production.

Attempts both in Britain and elsewhere to establish a sort of 'bespoke' motor cycle industry — selling expensive hand made machines of individualistic design have met with various difficulties. A few have been minimally successful. Some more ambitious ventures, such as Hesketh, have been failures. It would be unfair and premature to apply that epithet to the rotary engined Norton, but that company has had an uphill struggle. John Bloor's brave attempt to revive Triumph is too young to be judged.

In Britain at any rate, successive legislation has, in the 1990s, made it harder and harder to become a motor cyclist at all, and at the end of 1991, draconian rises in the cost of insurance look like accelerating motor cycling's decline.

In astonishing contrast is the interest of Britain and Europe in the 'classic movement' which was focussed by the publication in the late 1970s of the magazine *Classic Bike* and which has gathered momentum ever since. A whole new industry has arisen to service this interest. Perhaps one day from this will come a new motorcycle industry — who knows? Stranger things have happened as the 20th century enters its last decade.

Many different manufacturers supplied machines for military use. American M.P.s used the Harley-Davidson; BMW supplied their R35 (below) and R75 (right). Bottom: BSA were one of the major British suppliers, making both 350 and 500cc models. The Indian soldier is reclining on a Matchless G3/L, a 350cc ohv machine.

THE GREAT DESIGNERS

PERHAPS the first really famous design, if only because it was so bold, was Paul Kelecom's FN four-cylinder-in-line of 1904. At first of only 400cc, it had shaft drive but neither clutch nor gears. It was rapidly improved and enlarged, gained a clutch and gears and not only sold extensively in its native Belgium, but was exported to England and America. The first American 'in-line-four', the Pierce Arrow, was an acknowledged copy of an imported FN and started a tradition that embraced Henderson, ACE, Excelsior, Cleveland and Indian. The FN 4, latterly of 750cc and with chain final drive, was made until 1926. Nor was this Kelecom's only successful design.

In England, Alfred Scott virtually re-invented the Day-cycle (crankcase compression) two-stroke engine, developing it over several years into a small twin suitable for a motorcycle. First offered for sale in 1909, the 'two speed, two cylinder, two stroke' Scott was a design of remarkable integrity that sold steadily until the end of the 1920s. Indeed the engine layout lasted into the 1960s.

The air-cooled single-cylinder Levis two-stroke, designed by Howard (Bob) Newey and the Butterfield half-brothers, was the first downright practical and uncomplicated light-weight. It first appeared in 1911, became enormously successful and was the basis of Levis two-strokes until 1939. It was also very widely imitated and made under licence. The German Zundapp company paid it a wonderful compliment in 1921 when they copied it to the smallest detail — without acknowledgement. They subsequently copied Levis model changes year by year until 1926.

No such copying was involved in the Velocette two-stroke of 1913, designed by Percy Goodman. Velocette, too, continued to make excellent two-strokes until the Second World War. Goodman also designed the immortal overhead camshaft K series of Velocettes, which first appeared in 1925, and later, the 'high camshaft' series of MOV, MAC and MSS — 250cc, 350cc and 500cc. The 500cc Velocetter 'Thruxton' was still in production in 1970 — a design life of 37 years.

Other long-lived designs include the horizontal single-cylinder layout of Carlo Guzzi's Moto Guzzi of 1921, Adalberto Garelli's side-by-side split-single two-stroke of 1933 and Giovanni Marcellino's fore-and-aft split single Puch (with asymmetrical port timings) that stayed in production in one model or another from 1923 until the late 1960s.

However, very rarely is a design really and truly 'original'. Edward Turner is often credited with having 'invented' the even-firing vertical twin with his Triumph Speed Twin of 1937. This is nonsense. There had been dozens of such twins in the past, while Triumph themselves had made the 650cc Val Page designed 6/1 twin since 1933, and even that was probably inspired by designs by Herman Reeb that Horex in Germany had launched a year earlier as 600cc and 800cc ohc models for sidecar use. But Turner's 1937 design, though in no way radical, was so remarkably neat and compact, so simple to produce, and had such a good all-round performance, that it set a style that was to be copied by all. Development of Turner's design in its various versions, lasted for more than 40 years.

Turner, in fact, had earlier been responsible for another design that really did show originality — the 500cc overhead camshaft Ariel Square Four that was the sensation of the 1930 Motor Cycle Show. Its unique cylinder layout and coupled contra-rotating crankshafts were never copied in its lifetime, its production life spanning nearly thirty years. Its capacity was raised to 600cc and then, with a complete redesign, to 1000cc. Brilliant designer as he was, Turner proved an even greater success as a manager at Triumph, where his career was legendary.

Nothing like so flamboyant as Turner, though equally deserving of being remembered as a designer, was Val Page, who joined JAP in 1914 and, after the war, revitalised their range of engines before leaving in 1925 to join Ariel. Once again he laid down a series of designs that put Ariel on a par with any other manufacturer of the time. He helped Turner with the square four and then went to Triumph. There, he designed the 250cc, 350cc and 500cc range of ohv singles later restyled by Turner as the Tiger 70, Tiger 80 and Tiger 90 models. As earlier mentioned, he also designed the 650cc 6/1 twin. In 1936, Page moved to BSA, where again he drew up a range of eminently modern single cylinder engines, which included the original M23 Gold Star. He moved back to Ariel in 1939. His last design for them was the brilliant all-enclosed 250cc twin-cylinder Ariel Leader two-stroke and its sporting version, the Arrow. Very few designers in any country can have been so prolific and successful.

In 1919, J S Rasmussen's DKW factory in Saxony set Germany on the road to supremecy in the manufacture of two strokes between the wars. Original designs by Hugo Ruppe were developed and then superseded by those of Herman Weber. In 1931, the Swiss-born designer Arnold Zoller was called in to develop split-single DKW racing

Three great designers — Val Page (left), Bert Hopwood (right) and Edward Turner (centre) — photographed at Triumph in 1937.

George William Patchett (left) of McEvoy, FN and Jawa and Walter William Moore of Douglas, Norton and NSU.

machines with water cooling and piston-pump assisted (blown) induction. With patient development by August Prussing, the 'blown' DKW became insuperable in the 250cc class in European road racing in the 1930s.

Unlike Puch, whose Marcellino designed and developed racers had inspired DKW to call in Arnold Zoller, DKW did not sell split-single two-strokes for road use. Instead, they became the first in the world to market 'flat-top piston' two-strokes, using the Schnurle patents. Herman Weber was again the designer. His RT125 of 1937 set entirely new standards of two-stroke performance.

However, the RT 125's extraordinary claim to fame was that its design was copied post-war by BSA for their 125cc Bantam, by Harley Davidson, by JL0, by Yamaha, by Suzuki and by at least another half dozen firms in Russia and Eastern Europe. It even formed the basis of post war DKW and MZ racing machinery when Germany was re-admitted to international competition. Under the control of race chief Walter Kaaden, MZ went on to develop the first two-strokes to equal and then to surpass the specific power outputs of four-stroke engines. Today's all conquering racing two-strokes all derive from Kaaden's work at MZ.

Walter Moore designed a 500cc ohc racing engine for Norton, which won the 1927 Senior TT on its first outing. Thereafter, though, it proved disappointing, so when Moore left to join NSU in Germany and to design a similar engine for them, Norton's Joe Craig breathed over young Arthur Carroll's shoulder as he designed a new engine for 1931 — with which Tim Hunt that year 'did the double', winning both Junior and Senior TTs. So was born the Manx Norton, which in the next 18 seasons, was to win 28 TTs, not to mention uncounted Grand Prix races, quite apart from its myriad successes in the hands of private owners right into the 1960s and even beyond.

In post-war Italy, Giulio Carcano attained legendary stature with his designs and development for the Moto Guzzi racing team between 1948 and 1957, his masterpiece being the celebrated 500cc V8. But one Moto Guzzi design of that era, the 500cc in-line watercooled four-cylinder with shaft drive, raced in 1953 and 1954, was designed not by Carcano, but by Carlo Giannini. He, together with Pietro Remor, had been involved long before the war with the four-cylinder design that became the watercooled supercharged Rondine, later taken over by Gilera for the 1937 season.

Post war, Remor was to design first the 1947 air cooled 500cc four-cylinder Gilera, and then in 1950, the very similar four-cylinder MV. Credit for developing the Gilera must go to Franco Pasoni, and that for the MV to Arturo Magni. Remor left MV in 1953 and joined the obscure company Motom. But between 1958 and 1974, MV won the 500cc world championship no less than 17 times.

One cannot leave Italian designers without mentioning Moto Guzzi's Antonio Miccuchi, while Fabio Taglioni of Ducati will always be remembered for his desmodromic valve gear, first used in 1958. Until very recently, his advanced designs kept Ducati right at the forefront of the field with medium-to-large-capacity sporting twins.

Remor (left) with Gilera

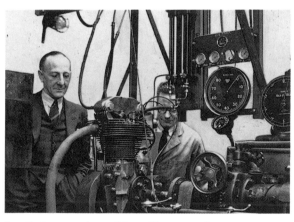

Joe Craig supervises a Manx Norton engine test. He was the architect of Norton's racing success for 25 years.

Fabio Taglioni (above) designed the Ducati desmodromic valve gear in the early 1960s. The system is still in use. Right: Giulio Carcano with Moto-Guzzi Junior TT winner in 1956.

Jack Williams, chief development engineer on the AJS 7R, with son-in-law Tom Herron, of Yamaha

Pioneer Max Friz . . . he made aircraft engines, then the first BMW motorcycle

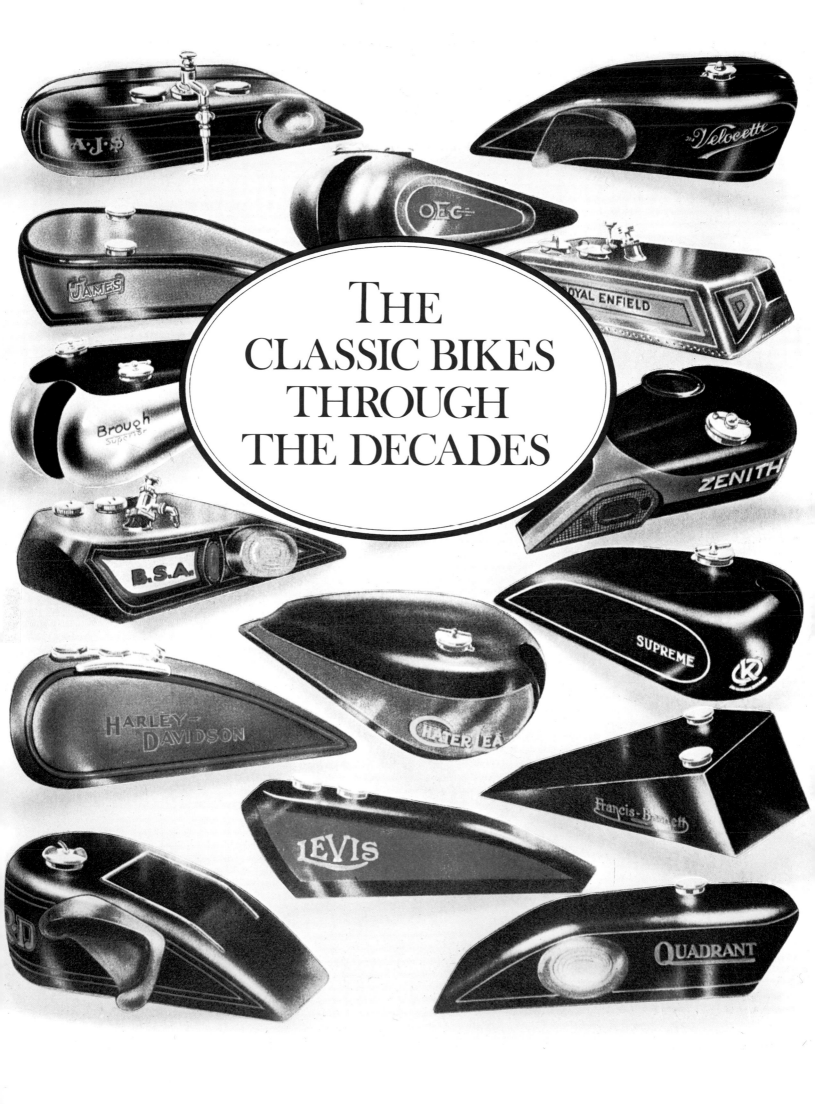

THE CLASSIC BIKES THROUGH THE DECADES

NO FOUR-CYLINDER MOTORCYCLE has achieved such pre-eminence in its own time as the Henderson. It provided riders in the early years of motorcycling with simple starting, smoothness, silence, oil tightness, reliability and generous power to a degree unmatched elsewhere. The model shown here is that of 1912, the first year of production. The original 7 hp model was soon further developed, with a multi-speed gearbox, improved power, and and more robust construction. Sales rose accordingly, and the model achieved greater popularity than any comparable machine in the United States. Finally, Ignaz Schwinn's Excelsior Company bought the firm in 1917, initially retaining the services of founders William and Tom

Henderson. After that, the Henderson big four also incorporated the name Excelsior on the tank. Two years later, William and Tom Henderson left Excelsior, unhappy with the new business arrangement. William founded his own motorcycle company, under the name of Ace. He was soon manufacturing an Ace four, and challenging the Henderson's reputation for quality. After many successful years Ace ran into financial troubles, and was bought by Indian.

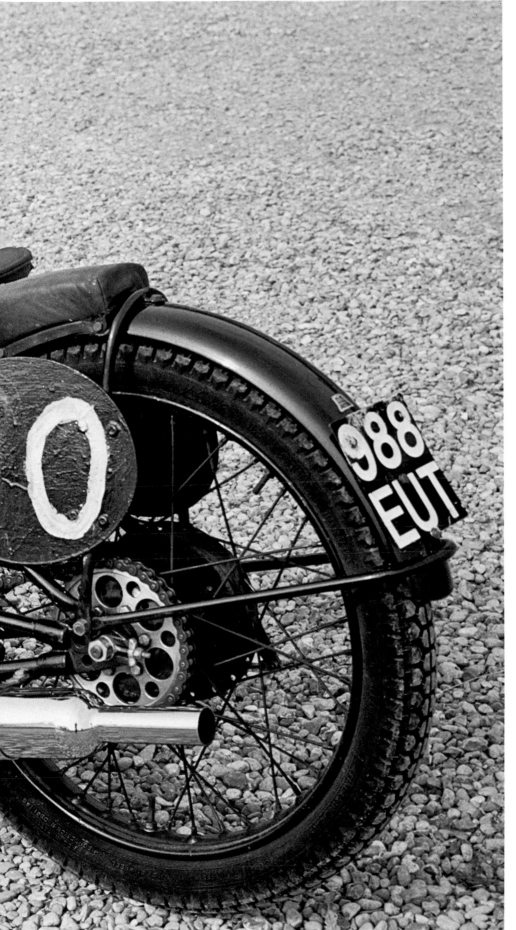

THE NAME SCOTT is central to the history of the motorcycle. Alfred Scott was an inventor and engine-designer who played a leading part in the development of the two-stroke machine. Scott built his first motorised bicycle in Yorkshire as early as 1898, using a twin-cylinder two-stroke. The engine was fitted to a heavy pedal-cycle, and transmission was by friction roller. By 1903, he had built a machine with rear-wheel power, and a year later Scott was granted British patent rights on a two-stroke vertical-twin engine. Scott's first true production motorcycle was manufactured in 1908. Its engine was built to the Scott design by the nearby Jowett car factory, another Yorkshire concern famous in automotive history. This 333cc engine had a bore and stroke of 58 × 63mm, and the entire unit weighed only 371 lbs. The cylinder heads were water-cooled through a thermosiphon system, but the barrels were air-cooled. By 1914, Scott had settled the design of his machines, and was using a wholly water-cooled engine. The two-speed machine had standard gear-ratios of 3:1 and 4:1, and the unusual "open" frame design which characterised the marque. This frame design was popular with women motorcyclists, whose dignity it helped preserve. Telescopic front forks were used from the very first, and a disc-valve induction and exhaust system was introduced at an early stage. Other machines could match the Scott's 55 mph top speed, but none of its contemporaries offered the same handling qualities. It was this characteristic in particular which afforded Scott such great racing success. Like most unconventional machines, the Scott was the creature of its designer. Alfred Scott himself left the company after the First World War, and died in 1923; within four or five years, the marque had lost much of its shine. Production since a takeover in 1950 has been limited to small-scale revivals. The Scott shown here is a 486cc model specially reconstructed for vintage racing.

INDIAN WAS WITHOUT DOUBT one of the foremost names in the development of the modern motorcycle. In 1905, the factory became one of the first to put a V-twin into commercial manufacture. The first V engine was little more than a doubling up of two Indian 1·75 hp singles, but improved and enlarged versions soon followed. These ultimately provided the basis for the very advanced motorcycles produced under the aegis of the factory's founder, George Hendee, and the great designer Oskar Hedström. After they had left the company, Charlie Gustafson became Indian's chief designer in 1915. He established the side-valve style which became a tradition of the factory and of the American motorcycle industry. His great machine

was the 7 hp 998 cc Power Plus shown here. This sophisticated and speedy motorcycle included such advanced equipment as leaf-spring suspended pivoted fork rear suspension, all chain drive, electric lighting, electric starting and a proper kick-start.

AS THE ORIGINAL William Brough motorcycle company entered the last year of its life, the son's rival firm launched the most famous machine to bear the family name. The Brough Superior SS100, introduced in 1925 was more popular than any other prestige sports roadster before or since. The SS100, shown here, was an overhead-valve V-twin. It became one of the two mainstays of Brough Superior's 19-year production period, along with its predecessor, the SS80 side-valve V-twin. As with all engines of its type, the side-valve twin was less durable at speed than the ohv. The '100' and '80' model designations referred to the machines' guaranteed top speed. Brough Superior was also known for a proliferation of multi-cylindered exotica.

The machines were largely assembled from proprietary components — the engines were principally JAP or Matchless units, and even the famous Castle forks were originally a Harley Davidson design. This philosophy was the Achilles' heel of Brough Superior.

The company tried unsuccessfully to develop its own power-units, and the cost of buying-in specially-manufactured engines in small quantities eventually proved to be crippling. The company stopped motorcycle production in 1940.

Brough Superior

SUNBEAM

THE SUNBEAM MODEL 90, shown on the right in its traditional black-and-gold livery, is probably the finest example of British single-cylinder engineering. It used simple, proven designs, with meticulous finish. The machine was conceived in 1923 as a sports roadster, and successfully adapted as a works racer. It was produced in both 350 and 500cc ohv versions. Production standards dropped after the factory was bought in 1930 by ICI (Imperial Chemical Industries). Sunbeam was later owned by Associated Motorcycles and BSA.

Douglas

ALTHOUGH DOUGLAS did sometimes use other engine layouts, the marque was always known for its horizontally-opposed twins. Today, Douglas is usually remembered for its post-war series of transverse-engined 350cc machines, but these were only made in the company's last seven years. In its earlier days, and for more than three decades, Douglas found its fame and fortune in exceptionally well-planned twins with a fore-and-aft arrangement. The success of these machines owed much to the work of the company's chief development rider, Freddie Dixon, during the middle and late 1920s. Fate also played a part. When the Douglas EW series of 350sv racers began to find the competition tough, Douglas had planned a new ohc model, but a fire at the works destroyed the blueprints and set back the company's work. The new engine was abandoned, and the company chose instead to give a new life to its old ohv twins, with considerable development work by Dixon. By happy chance, these machines proved most successful in the newly-arrived sport of speedway. Some of their success was due to a freak of design which led the frame to flex during broadsliding, but their achievements on the cinder track boosted all aspects of the Douglas reputation. During this period, the classic Douglas machine was the model FW, which was produced in 500cc and 600cc versions. The road-racing version is shown here. The road-racing models were capable of 90 mph and 95 mph respectively. In 1929 alone, 1300 machines were sold.

Rudge

SOME OF THE BEST British production bikes were replicas of their makers' works racing models. A fine example was the 1929 Rudge-Whitworth Ulster, which came from a factory famous for its advanced approach. The machine was introduced to celebrate Graham Walker's win in the Ulster Grand Prix, and it proved to be exceptionally fast and reliable. It had a four-speed positive-stop, foot-change gearbox, dry sump lubrication with a mechanical pump, and a four-valve cylinder head in a penthouse combustion chamber.

THE BRITISH EXCELSIOR company is remembered with affection for a 250cc single which was popularly known as the "Mechanical Marvel," but this four-valve ohv machine suffered from its own complexity. Undaunted, Excelsior continued along the same development path with an improved four-valver, the famous Manxman, shown here. This machine had a single overhead camshaft, and each inlet valve was fed by its own Amal RN carburettor. The bronze head, as shown, improved thermal efficiency in the days before aluminium had come into common use. The Manxman shown is a 250, but a 350 was also produced. Valve gear and carburettor tune still proved "very pernickerty" according to Excelsior's managing director Eric Walker, and in 1938 the firm introduced two-valve engines. These were equally fast, but wholly reliable. They had sprung frames, and proved so successful that they continued to be raced in private hands into the early 1950s.

OTHER SINGLE-CYLINDER machines may have exemplified a particular aspect of engineering or of performance, but those produced by Velocette demonstrated the full range of attributes. This was best accomplished by the KTT (left), a racing replica of the works' own grand prix machinery, which was also notable as the first model to sport the Velocette-perfected foot gear-change system. This was an ohc

single of 350cc, sold with a guaranteed top speed of 85 mph. As an option, Velocette offered a 100 mph dope-tuned model sporting a 9:1 compression ratio. The range ran from the 1929 Mk 1 illustrated here to the 1949 Mk VIII. In 1956, Velocette demonstrated its skills with a quite different range of well-remembered singles. These were ohv sports roadsters. First came the 499cc Venom, shown above, with a "square" (86 × 86mm) engine, then the smaller 349cc Viper. The Venom engine developed 36 bhp at 6,200 rpm, giving the machine a top speed of 95 mph. After 12 and 24-hour records had been set at Montlhéry, a highly-tuned version was produced as a clubman racer. This was the Thruxton (right), which had a top speed of approximately 120 mph.

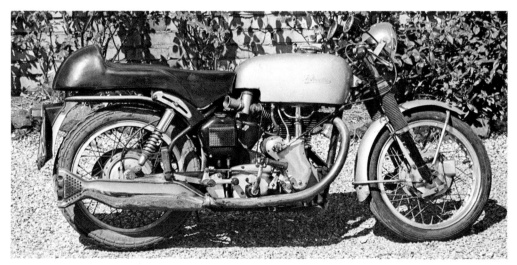

BSA

FOR MOST OF ITS LIFE, the BSA marque was known primarily for singles of simple and inexpensive design, made for everyday transport. The motorcycles in the small picture are examples: a 250cc machine from 1925 (background) and the 1928 "Sloper". In later years, the same qualities of durability and reliability were showcased in a much more exotic motorcycle, the Gold Star. No clubman racer has ever enjoyed the success or reputation of the "Goldie". The range was produced in trial, scramble, touring and racing versions, and a 1959 model of the latter is shown here. The 500cc engine developed up to 40 bhp at just over 7,000 rpm, through a close ratio gearbox. Top speed was around 120 mph in full clubman trim.

HARLEY–DAVIDSON

THE HARLEY-DAVIDSON Electra-Glide has its origins in the SV 74 twin of 1922, although its more recent and direct ancestor is the first ohv 1200 of 1941. These early machines displayed the familiar styling features of most American motorcycles: leading link front forks, solid rear wheel mounting, pan saddles, footboards, high, wide handle-bars, and a V-twin engine, all of which produce comfort at low cruising speeds. Over the years, the range has been modernised and renamed, but the essential concept has remained the same. In 1949, the Hydra-Glide was introduced with a telescopic front fork. The next model, with pivoted-fork rear suspension, produced in 1959, was the Duo-Glide. With the addition of a starter motor in 1965 came the name Electra-Glide. Since then, little has changed except the adoption of cast alloy wheels, although numerous Japanese components, such as forks and carburettor, have been adopted. The Electra-Glide is the heaviest mass-produced motorcycle ever built, weighing 800 lbs fully equipped. The 45°, 1207cc V-twin has hydraulically-activated push-rods and produces 62 bhp at 5,200 rpm, and 70ft/lbs of torque at 4,000 rpm. The XLCR (below, kitted out for the track) has similarly won cult status among the world's army of Harley fanatics. The classic sporting Harley, the XLCR was launched in 1976; it is the fastest production bike Harley-Davidson have ever built, with a flat out top speed of a good 120mph. What this, and subsequent Harleys are about — currently the regular 1340cc Evolution series engines arc fitted to a range of 17 different bikes — is big vee-twin power, image and style.

THERE ARE MANY REASONS for celebrating the famous marque founded by Howard R. Davies (hence its original name, HRD) and bought shortly afterwards by Philip Vincent. Modern motorcycle manufacturers have still barely caught up with the progressive chassis-group designs produced by Vincent 35 years ago, though the marque is more commonly remembered for its spree of speedy achievement during the 1950s. Perhaps these sporting feats were the inspiration for the unusually-large and ambitious speedo which was fitted to Vincent motorcycles. Factory and private riders captured national and world speed and sprint records by the

handful on the competition model of the period, the Black Lightning. The word "Black" featured in the names of several famous Vincent machines. One unsupercharged Black Lightning achieved a speed of 185·15 mph in the hands of Russell Wright, a New Zealander, in 1955. Sadly, this was also the last year of full production.

The firm went out in a blaze of glory, with the announcement of the semi-streamlined Series D models, but few were actually made. In design, these machines were the natural successors to the Series C Rapides, which had been launched in 1949, with 50-degree 998cc V-twin engines. The Series C standard touring machine provided a top speed of approximately 105/110 mph, and its sporting counterpart the Black Shadow (shown here) went to 110/120 mph, reaching 56 mph in only six seconds. These machines were in turn developed from the Series A Rapides, which were launched in 1937, had 47-degree engines, and had a web of external pipes.

ARIEL was in every sense an historic British marque. Established since 1898, the firm exhibited all the characteristics of British motorcycle manufacture. The products were well made, even sporty, but initially of conventional design. In 1929, a much more sophisticated machine made a considerable break with tradition. This was a 500cc four with a highly-unusual "square" cylinder configuration and single overhead camshaft. This distinctive engine layout became so identifiable with the marque that the nickname "Squariel" passed into the language of motorcycling. Like the later Triumph Speed Twin, another pace-setting machine, the Square

Four was designed by Edward Turner. It had an all ball-and-roller bearing engine and horizontally-split crankcase. In 1931, the engine was bored out from 51 to 56 mm, thus increasing capacity to 600cc. Although some modest success was achieved in competition, such as the Bickel

brothers' supercharged 111·42 lap at Brooklands in 1934, the machine was really a sporting tourer. In 1936, Ariel launched a 1,000cc Square Four of quite new engine design. This model had a pushrod power-unit, with plain bearings, and it also utilised a unique trailing-link rear-suspension system. It remained in production in various roadster forms until the late 1950s, by which time it boasted four individual exhaust-pipes ports and an all-aluminium engine. The 1956 luxury roadster shown here develops 42 bhp at 5,800 rpm, providing a top speed of 105 mph. It has a bore and stroke of 65 × 75 mm. The machine's kerb-weight is 495 lbs.

TRIUMPH

TRIUMPH WILL ALWAYS be associated with the vertical-twin engine-layout. This classic design was introduced in 1938, in the 498cc Speed Twin, which was the fore-runner of many famous motorcycles. A memorable example was the larger Thunderbird (above), introduced in 1949. This 649cc tourer produced 34 bhp at 6,000 rpm on a compression ratio of 7:1. Three standard models averaged 101·06 mph between them for 500 miles at Montlhéry. A total break with the vertical-twin layout came in the 1960s with the transverse three-cylinder Trident (left). The T160 had a 740cc engine of 67 × 70 mm bore and stroke, giving 58 bhp at 7,250 rpm to reach a top speed of around 120 mph. Production ended in the mid-1970s.

Norton

IT WAS THE GREAT racing success of the Norton marque which created the need for an improved frame in the 1940s. The need was met by the McCandless brothers' Featherbed frame, which in turn influenced motorcycle design almost everywhere. After being introduced on the Manx racers, the Featherbed frame was modified for road use in the existing 497cc tourer, which became the Dominator in 1952. The example shown above is a Manx built in 1958. Ten years after its launch, the Dominator had grown to 647cc, with a maximum road speed of 112 mph. In 1965, Norton launched the 745cc Atlas, but a more significant development came two years later. The same engine was fitted, with rubber mountings, into a new duplex frame. This new model, the Commando, was subsequently increased in size to 828cc. With a top speed of 120 mph, the Commando (bottom) is the most powerful road-going Norton ever produced.

LIKE THE LAMBORGHINI CAR, the equally exotic Laverda is the product of an Italian agricultural engineering group. With its race-bred frame and sleek styling, the 130 mph RGS 1000 (below) is Laverda's flagship. It is derived from the Laverda Jota, which with a top speed of 150 mph verified in independent tests, was the fastest production roadster ever built. The RGS 1000 is powered by a 981cc three-cylinder motor which features 120° crankshaft and gives 80 bhp.

THE MV AGUSTA AMERICA is arguably the finest sports roadster in production, and without doubt a classic among the multicylindered big bikes. The entire power-unit is a development of the company's racing 500cc four of the 1950s. MV was the last European marque to dominate the Grand Prix circuits, and retired solely for commercial reasons, but it took several attempts before the factory's sporting experience could be translated into a successful roadster. The 788cc dohc America develops 75 bhp at 8,500 rpm, and its top speed is approximately 135 mph.

MOTO GUZZI

WHILE JAPANESE motorcycles have become increasingly sophisticated, the largest of the Italian manufacturers has responded by offering machines of comparable performance but robust simplicity. The V 850 GT of 1972 typifies Moto Guzzi's approach. The transverse twin turns out 64·5 bhp at a mere 6,500 rpm, providing a top speed of 115 mph. In 1975, the entire range was expanded to include the revolutionary V 1,000, with hydraulic torque converter.

DUCATI

IT WAS BUILT for its high-speed handling, apparently with no other priority in mind, and in this respect the Ducati Desmo 864cc of 1975 has no serious rival. Its top speed is 135 mph, its kerb weight a mere 428 lbs, and it is a remarkably stable motorcycle. The machine also benefits from the efficiency and reliability of the desmodromic valve system. Only Ducati has used this system with total success. The technique was employed to great effect in the 1972 750 SS clubman racer, after being first introduced by the factory's chief engineer, Fabioni Taglioni, in the successful Grand Prix period which was during the late 1950s.

BMW PREACHED THE virtues of conservatism in motorcycle design for decades, preferring to rely on tried and tested engineering, rather than embark on innovation for innovation's sake. The flat twin concept, for long favoured by the company, dated back to the 1930s, for instance; the R100RS (main picture), the classic BMW of the mid-1970s onwards, changed relatively little over the years. Though aerodynamically the machine was very advanced — the result of concentrated fairing development involving elaborated wind tunnel testing — the engine was a practical and simple horizontally-opposed 980cc ohv twin, producing 70bhp at 7,000 rpm and a top speed of around 125mph. Contrast this with the revolutionary K1 (inset), which BMW launched in 1989. This striking, sensa-

tional looking machine was designed to meet and beat the Japanese competition. Its distinctive bodywork is designed for absolute aerodynamic efficiency, while its engine is an improved 16-valve version of the four-cylinder K100 engine of 1984. The combus-tion chambers were reworked and the crankshaft, con rods and pistons lightened, so the unit revved harder, while the machine also utilises the Bosch Motoronic digital engine management system, as fitted to BMW cars. Top speed is 149mph.

THE CBR1000 (main picture) is Honda's flagship sports roadster. Launched in 1987, the machine triumphantly fulfills the brief Honda gave its designers — to produce a 1000cc open class sports bike for the road rider that was powerful, comfortable and smooth to ride and sophisticated in appearance. The CBR1000's success underlines Honda's decades of experience in building in-line fours. The bike exudes confidence, balance and completeness. It is a road rider's machine par excellence, with an excellent riding position, plenty of room for a pillion and luggage and, between your legs, a short stroke, 16 valve in-line four that will pull top gear from 2000rpm. The power output is smooth, with no discernible vibration except at the top of the rev range, where there is a real top end rev

thrust. The ST1100 Pan-European (inset) is another Honda beauty. What distinguishes it from its stablemates is that, although built in Japan, it was the first Honda to be designed and styled in Europe. Launched in 1990, it is every inch a sports-touring flagship. It comes with a large, spacious saddle, a big full fairing and windscreen, an ample fuel tank, a comfortable riding position and a large 1084cc vee-four engine, specially built for long distance reliability.

YAMAHA'S 1989 FZR-750R (OWO1) (top picture) looks exactly what it is — a mean racing machine. It is available for road use only because the factory had to build over 1000 examples to qualify the bike to compete in World Super-Bike racing. It built on the success of the established FZR1000 (above), which, since its launch in 1987 has become an industry classic. The design is an object lesson in the mating of a hugely powerful engine to a

strong, yet fairly light and fast-responding, chassis, the result being a bike that, although undeniably a pure sports machine, is one of the very best road bikes available, as worldwide sales confirm. Top speed of the 1989 Exup variant is an official 172mph.

⚡ SUZUKI

SUKUKI'S ENTRY INTO the four-stroke super-bike arena started back in 1977 with the GS750; the line continued with the GSX1100E Katana (main picture). The company also dominated the two-stroke scene with their RG500, which, in its heyday, took the manufacturer's championship for seven consecutive seasons. Suzuki's current two-stroke contender is the RGV500 (right), a trim-looking Vee 4 that was launched in 1987 and has been steadily refined and improved ever since. Experts claim its biggest asset is its quick handling, achieved by taking weight off the front wheel and shifting the compact engine rearwards in the frame. The engine design, however, has posed problems; the RGV has suffered from ignition, crankshaft and piston failures though Suzuki is confident that these problems will be resolved sooner rather than later.

Kawasaki

KAWASAKI'S QUEST FOR speed made it the first manufacturer in the world to offer fuel-injection as a production standard, as in the GPZ1100 (top); today, the ZZ-R1100 (above) is the only mass-production motor cycle with a top speed genuinely in excess of 170mph. Launched in 1990, it currently dominates the super—bike scene, one reason for this being the use of a ram-air intake system, based on Formula One car technology. The faster the machine goes, the more air it rams in, with more airflow, power and speed as a result. Its stable-mate, the ZXR750 (right), was launched in 1989 as a race replica for the road. It features a proven roadster engine, itself extensively revised in 1990, in a race-orientated chassis. The result — a very fine sports roadster.

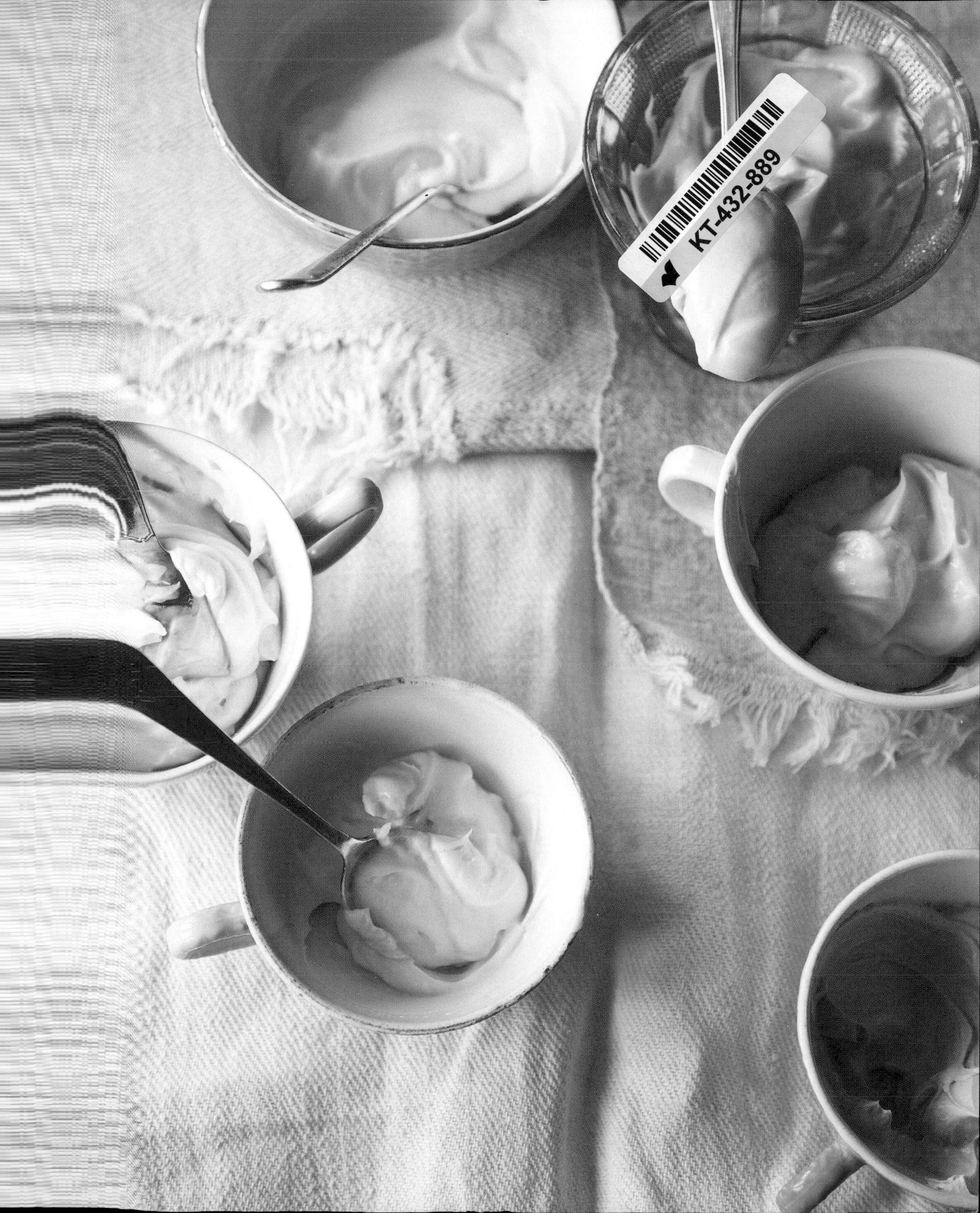

CELEBRATION
CAKES

FIONA CAIRNS

photographs by Laura Edwards

quadrille

KT-432-889

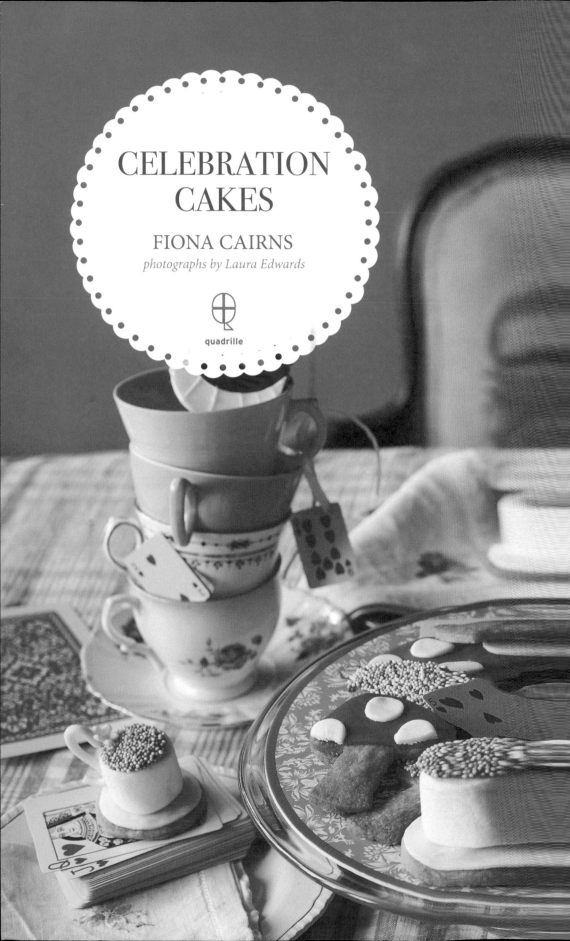

CELEBRATION CAKES

FIONA CAIRNS

photographs by Laura Edwards

quadrille

CELEBRATION
CAKES

FIONA CAIRNS

photographs by Laura Edwards

quadrille

To my parents Monty and Kaye, with love and thanks for all your support

To Mary Doody, whose birthday cakes make more people's days than anyone else I know

The Cakes

Gingerbread cottage
Cinnamon-orange gingerbread
Russian dolls
Lime and vodka syrup cake
Black Forest bombe
Chocolate kirsch cake

✶ VAMPIRE PARTY ✶
*Devil's cardamom chocolate cake,
   Chocolate shortbread*

Bridge tray bake
Coffee cake
Turkish delight meringue
Strawberry and elderflower cake
Playing dice
Banoffee cake
Jewel box
Australian panforte
Robots
Crispy Mars Bar fridge cake

✶ VINTAGE TEA PARTY ✶
*Madeira cake, Earl Grey fairy
   cakes, Rose and violet creams*

Chewy, gooey, nutty caramel bars
Very lemony meringue cake
All-in-one lemon cake
Flourless lemon polenta cake
with limoncello syrup
Eastern tile mosaic
Apricot-cardamom cake
Pistachio, Grand Marnier and
   olive oil cake
Box of chocolates
Sachertorte

Erupting volcano
Marble cake
Chocolate dinosaurs
Sugar fossils
Peanut-choc caramel cookies
Football boots
All-in-one chocolate cake
Little monsters
All-in-one orange cake
Mojito and Piña Colada
   cheesecakes
Pirate galleon
Giant jam sandwich biscuits
Fresh flower heart
Beside the seaside - a bucket cake
Neapolitan sponge
Over the rainbow
Hidden fruit and veg cakes

✶ ALICE IN WONDERLAND'S
UNBIRTHDAY PARTY ✶
Madeira cake, Vanilla shortbread

Fairies on fairy cakes
Rhubarb and anise crumble cake
Piggy bank
Victoria sponge
Blackberry, lavender, rose and
   white chocolate cake
Angel surprise cake
Angel cake
Marzipan fruits hat
Easiest ever all-in-one fruit cake
Pastel ice cream sandwiches
Bejewelled elephant
A fantasy castle
Toffee cake

Blueberry yogurt cupcakes
Spun sugar pile
Liquorice toffee cake
Merry-go-round
Coconut and chocolate
   stripy cake
Toffee apple pops
Marmalade syrup cake

✶ GLAMPING PARTY ✶
*Spiced apple cake, Almond lemon
   biscuits, Brownies*

Tiramisu cake
Glazed chocolate-orange cubes
Orange sachertorte
Liquorice toffee cupcakes

✶ A GARDENER'S DELIGHT ✶
Elderflower and lemon cakes

Butterscotch cake
Allergen-free chocolate cake
Savoury smoked salmon 'cake'
All-in-one apricot and
   almond cake
Bakewell tart
Nectar cake
Honey cake
Masala chai cake

✶ DECORATING KEY ✶
🕯 = easy
🕯🕯 = some effort required
🕯🕯🕯 = challenging

Every day of the year is a chance to celebrate, whether for someone's birthday, with close friends or family, or a big occasion that warrants a large bash. A cake is the centrepiece, often ablaze with candles, cut with a secret wish and shared to create precious memories.

In these pages you will find many delicious recipes and ideas, designed to take the stress out of wondering what to bake. Of course you don't need to wait for a celebration to come along; make any day of the year special and let the cake itself become the occasion.

We all have our own memories of lovely cakes baked for us, and many families have a treasured recipe, made for every occasion. Perhaps you'll find a new family favourite in these pages. I still remember the delight I felt when my mother presented me with a sugary pink crinoline doll cake... I must have been about six! In making a celebration cake, you are creating something far more than the cake itself. By putting in your time and effort you will give joy and delight and make someone's day extra special. That warm memory will remain long after every crumb has disappeared.

You will find something for everyone, from children to centenarians and plenty in between. Over the years I have often struggled to think of celebration cake ideas for men, and you will find plenty of the solutions I have come up with here.

With each of the five themed parties – from Alice in Wonderland for little girls to a vegetable plot for the older among us – you will find little biscuits and cakes. Either make these to accompany the main celebration cake, or instead of the big cake, or even offer them as little gifts, packed into bags to be taken home by guests.

But there is an important ingredient missing from these recipes. When selecting what cake you will make, doing the shopping, gathering ingredients together, baking, icing and decorating your creation, do so with love and enjoyment and not out of duty and full of anxiety. Stir in happy thoughts while you make the batter, and remember the great pleasure you are going to give to the people sharing in the day's celebration.

If you are stressed and baking is a chore, it will somehow transpose into the cake mix. While I was writing this book, a friend dropped by. I was baking a cake for the third time, and not too successfully. I think she was hoping there might be some delicious cake hanging around, but instead she found me having a bad day and no cake in sight. 'It'll get into the cakes; go and do something else for a while,' she said. Very wise words that I have not forgotten.

My advice is to try not to seek perfection. Find something in this book that you have the time to make and feel confident about. If cake decorating is all relatively new to you, then don't be too ambitious. Frankly I don't think it matters if a cake is slightly imperfect and doesn't look like the photo. I'm sure it's nothing a bit of extra icing, decoration and candles won't fix. A very simple cake, freshly baked, with festive candles is hard to beat. It doesn't have to be complicated to be a success. There are some wonderful recipes here that are undecorated but still celebratory and, of course, completely delicious. With practice you'll soon be amazed at what you are able to produce. That said, there are plenty of more elaborate ideas here too for all ages, with clear instructions, which can be followed exactly. If you are more experienced, use these directions only as guidelines and create something even more exquisite.

Apart from choosing a cake that is suitable to you, do remember it should be appropriate for the recipient and, if you can, try to personalise it: mark out their age with candles (if there are not too many, that is!); their name; or their favourite flavours or colours.

The last thing to bear in mind is that a cake needs to fit the occasion. A cake for a children's birthday party is very different to a cake for a girlie afternoon tea, or a cake served at the end of a dinner party.

Whatever type of party you are throwing (or even if there isn't one), I hope this book will inspire you and fire your imagination.

Remember, stir in the happy thoughts, enjoyment and love.

Ingredients

STORE CUPBOARD

* baking powder
* bicarbonate of soda
* chocolate
  —*55% cocoa solids chocolate*
  —*70% cocoa solids chocolate*
  —*milk chocolate*
* cocoa powder
* cornflour
* eggs, large, free-range
* flours
  —*plain*
  —*self-raising*
* golden syrup
* ground almonds
* jams and spreads
  —*apricot jam*
  —*dulce de leche*
  (or caramel spread)
  —*lemon curd*
  —*strawberry jam*
* oranges
* rose water
* sea salt
* spices
  —*cardamom pods*
  —*ground cinnamon*
  —*ground ginger*
* sugar
  —*dark muscovado*
  —*golden caster*
  —*icing*
  —*light muscovado*
  —*white caster*
* sunflower oil
* unsalted butter
* unwaxed lemons
* vanilla
  —*extract*
  —*pods*
  —*sugar*

BUTTER
I usually use unsalted butter for baking and make sure it really is soft... but not melted, of course, unless specified in the recipe. If butter is creamed to my instructions, it produces light cakes with excellent flavour.

CHOCOLATE
These recipes indicate the percentage of cocoa solids in the dark chocolate used. For milk chocolate, use at least 30% cocoa solids. And buy good Swiss white chocolate, which is best for cooking and making ganaches.

EGGS
Choose large organic or free-range eggs.

FLOUR
Unbleached, stoneground flour has the best flavour.

NUTS
Buy little and often as they turn rancid quickly. Any leftover nuts freeze brilliantly. Always roast nuts before using, to release the oils and improve the flavour.

ROSE WATER AND ORANGE FLOWER WATER
The better brands tend to be more intense. Add gradually to taste, as some bottles are double strength.

SPICES
Buy small amounts of whole spices and store in the dark. Grind them as needed; the flavour is incomparable to pre-ground.

SUGAR
Golden caster and muscovado sugars have the best flavours, both of butterscotch and of the molasses clinging to the grains.

VANILLA
I adore real vanilla (though it doesn't come cheap) and use vanilla seeds when I can instead of extract (do not buy vanilla flavour, whatever you do). A vanilla pod is the equivalent of about 2 tsp extract. Get into the habit of keeping vanilla sugar: a few whole or scraped pods in a sealed jar of caster sugar. It is invaluable for baking, imparting wonderful flavour.

Baking Tips

BAKING PARCHMENT
I use non-stick baking parchment for lining tins. It is vital for meringues; they stick to greaseproof paper.

BE PREPARED
Always think ahead, and gather all ingredients and equipment together before you start. Make sure you have read the recipe right through to the very end. For baking, ensure that all ingredients are at room temperature.

BISCUITS
Always flour your work surface and rolling pin, and have a palette knife to move the biscuits. If biscuit dough is too soft it will be impossible to handle, and if it has chilled for too long it will be too hard. Once the dough is rolled, you can chill it for 15 minutes. It should then cut like a dream. Cut out shapes very closely together, as the more you re-roll the offcuts, the tougher the biscuits will be.

FREEZING
In an ideal world I wouldn't freeze cakes as nothing beats a cake freshly baked from the oven. But I realise that life doesn't always make this possible, and you may well need to plan ahead. Freeze cakes un-iced and ice them when defrosted. Buttercream can be frozen separately.

KNOW YOUR OVEN
In baking, it is vital your oven should run at the temperature to which it is set. It is surprisingly common how often they don't. Invest in an oven thermometer, to check.

PAPER CASES
Confusingly, the sizes and names vary. As a general rule, very small cases are called 'petit four' or 'mini-muffin'. The next size up are often called 'bun' or 'fairy cake', then 'cupcake', and the largest 'muffin'.

SCORCHING, AND HOW TO AVOID IT
If a cake is cooking too quickly and developing a dark crust on top, make a foil cover a bit larger than the cake, tear a hole in the centre, open it up and place over the cake. This protects the edges of the top surface.

SPHERICAL CAKES
If you invest in the spherical tin (used for my Teapot and Piggy Bank, see pages 99 and 109), use it. Try making a fish bowl, a football, a globe or even a ball covered in flowers.

EQUIPMENT
* airtight containers
* baking parchment, *non-stick*
* baking trays
* bowls, *including heatproof bowls*
* cake tins; *a selection*
* craft knife
* cupcake trays, *in different sizes*
* cutters, *in different sizes and shapes*
* electric mixer and/or food processor *(optional)*
* hand-held electric whisk
* lemon squeezer
* measuring jug
* measuring spoons
* mini hole baking trays
* mortar and pestle
* oven thermometer
* paint brushes; *a selection*
* palette knife
* paper cases: *bun, cupcake, mini muffin, muffin*
* pastry brush *(not nylon)*
* piping bag, *large nylon*
* plastic disposable icing bags
* polythene bags
* rolling pins, *large and small*
* saucepans; *a selection*
* scales, *preferably digital*
* scissors
* sharp knives; *a selection*
* sieve
* skewers, *metal and wooden*
* spatula
* spoons, *metal and wooden*
* star nozzles, *in different sizes*
* storage tins
* tea towels; *lots of!*
* wire cooling racks
* work boards – *wooden, plastic and marble – in different sizes*
* zester

Icings

To clear up any confusion, I thought I'd list the icings I've used throughout the book.

BUTTERCREAM
Delicious and very easy to make, this can be flavoured in so many different ways. If it has become too hard (if it has been made a day or so previously, or has been frozen and defrosted), simply re-whisk it with a drop or two of boiling water to make it really creamy.

FONDANT (POWDER)
I have only used this once in this book (for Tiny Rose and Violet Creams, see page 55). It can be used to ice cakes too and is available from specialist cake decorating suppliers. It is soft, like the centre of a fondant fancy (so do not confuse it with sugarpaste, which is sometimes confusingly called rolled fondant).

GLACE ICING
The simplest of the lot, this is simply sieved icing sugar, a liquid – water, lemon juice, rose water – and maybe a colour. It can be drizzled over a batch of small cakes (as in Fairies on Fairy Cakes, see page 105) or a large cake. Easy to control, to thin it out add more liquid, or to thicken, more icing sugar.

MEXICAN MODELLING PASTE
This sets very hard and is great for fine modelling. Mix with sugarpaste to make it more pliable.

ROYAL ICING
1 egg white
250g icing sugar, sifted, plus more if needed

Whisk the egg white until bubbles appear. Then whisk in the sugar a little at a time. Continue to whisk for one to two minutes, remembering it must hold its shape when piped. Gradually add water to thin, or icing sugar to thicken.
Royal icing is invaluable both to stick decorations together and for piping detail. It will store in the fridge for a week in a sealed container.

SUGARPASTE
Now widely available in the supermarkets. I don't think it is worth making this yourself. Always knead sugarpaste before use; it will become pliable and cover your cakes with a smooth professional finish. You will always need to start with more than you need when covering a cake. (You can seal any clean offcuts in a polythene bag and re-use them.)
Sugarpaste is great for making decorations, just like children's modelling clay. You can buy it ready coloured, or colour your own more interesting shades. Sugarpaste has three enemies: it hates the fridge; drops of water scar it; airtight containers make it 'sweat'. It does dry out fairly quickly, so once you are working with it, don't go off and do something else! Keep sugarpaste sealed in polythene bags when not in use, to stop it drying out.
When rolling out sugarpaste, dust a work surface and rolling pin with icing sugar, and be sure to run a palette knife frequently under the paste, to stop it sticking to the surface.
If colouring sugarpaste, especially to cover a cake, try to do so the day before required. The colour will intensify slightly overnight. This is especially important if you are making a dark colour, as it will become much more manageable after it has rested. To colour sugarpaste, see page 168.
Get ahead and make sugarpaste (and petal and modelling paste) decorations in advance. Stored in cardboard boxes, they keep for weeks, even months.

WHITE PETAL PASTE
Use this to make delicate flowers, as it can be rolled very thinly. The paste dries quickly, so you need to work fast.

...AND FILLING PIPING BAGS
Whatever you are using – royal icing, buttercream or simply melted chocolate – do not ever over-fill a bag; you'll make a mess! Aim to fill a bag only half full.

Decorating Tips

Either follow my recipes to the letter, or don't! The ideas in this book can be copied exactly, or used purely to fire your own imagination and creativity. I hope you find the instructions clear. Here are a few tips to help you along the way.

COPY FROM LIFE
Something I always find invaluable is to find the real article to copy if appropriate. If you can find a real football boot, Russian doll, rose or pear, it will make your sugar creation all the more convincing.

COVERING CAKES
Never cover a cake that is even slightly warm with any kind of icing or sugarpaste. It must be completely cold.

EDIBLE GLUE
In this book, I've often used edible glue (from cake decorating suppliers, see page 188) instead of royal icing to stick decorations to cakes. Use it in moderation; you really only need a touch.

FOOD COLOURS
As a rule, do use food colour paste as opposed to the more readily available liquids. You won't need to use too much, unless you are mixing a strong colour. If you try to use liquid food colour with sugarpaste, it will become too sticky and you won't get the intensity of colour anyway. Sometimes I do get a bit carried away mixing up colours... it comes from years of painting, I suppose!
Recently, at last, you can buy natural food colours in liquid form in some supermarkets. I have used them very successfully to make my Over the Rainbow cakes (see page 94) in very pretty pastel colours. Natural colours have two drawbacks: they are light sensitive, so they need to be eaten quickly before the colours oxidise; and if you use them to make strong, bright colours they may flavour the icing itself, so use them with care and discretion (paprika-flavoured icing is most definitely not good!).

GLITTERS
There is a whole rainbow of edible glitters available, though I tend to use clear glitter. Even just a few highlights can lift a whole decorating scheme.

INSTANT FLAT SURFACE
It is far easier to decorate a cake if you simply turn it upside down, so the domed surface is underneath.

RIBBONS
To wrap a ribbon around a board, it is best to use double-sided tape for the most professional finish. When placing a ribbon around a cake be careful, as dots of royal icing will show through and spoil the look of the cake. Try to use as little as possible and, if you can, attach the join only at the back of the cake.

STURDY BASES
I use thin cake card, cake board (stronger and thicker) and cake drums (give height and even more strength) to support cakes. Sometimes I cut a cake card to shape under a cake to make it easier to move the cake. It becomes invisible under the sugarpaste (for instance for the Crocodile Handbag, see page 51).

STORAGE
The great advantage of a cake covered with sugarpaste is that it is sealed, so will keep, if stored in dry conditions, very well for a few days. If it has buttercream underneath this is fine. However, if the icing contains cream or cream cheese it should be in the fridge. Therefore, if using the latter, remember you can't cover the cake and leave it at room temperature to get ahead by a couple of days. Sugarpaste put in the fridge is a bad idea; it will become sticky.

A NOTE ON ALTERNATIVE CAKES
Throughout the book, I suggest other cake flavours to go underneath decoration schemes. These are only suggestions; other recipes may work well, too. Please remember that alternative recipe suggestions may need different baking times and cake tin sizes.

Gingerbread Cottage
CINNAMON-ORANGE GINGERBREAD

TO BAKE

700g plain flour, plus more
   to dust
4 tsp ground ginger
2 tsp ground cinnamon
2 tsp bicarbonate of soda
250g salted butter, very slightly
   softened and diced
3 egg yolks
200g light muscovado sugar
6 tbsp golden syrup
finely grated zest of 1 orange

SPECIAL EQUIPMENT

wall, roof, base and door
   templates (see page 17)
3cm heart cutter
1.5cm circle cutter (or the end
   of a piping nozzle)

There's no reason why a gingerbread house should be reserved for Christmas festivities and covered in snow. It makes a great cake at any time of the year, personalised with favourite sweets or chocolates. It will keep for up to a week, stored in a dry place.

TO BAKE

Sift the flour, spices and bicarbonate of soda into a large bowl and add the butter. Rub together with your fingertips – or tip into a food processor or the bowl of an electric mixer and blend – until the mixture resembles fine crumbs.

Add the egg yolks, sugar, syrup and orange zest and mix until the dough comes together. If it's too sticky, add a little more flour.

Wrap in cling film and chill for at least an hour to rest the dough. Line two or three baking trays with baking parchment.

Divide the dough in half. Roll out one half on a well-floured surface into a large rectangle about 5mm thick. Cut out two rectangles for the roof, each 15.5x21cm; it cuts like a dream! (Or lift the rolled out dough on to the baking sheets and cut it to shape there.)

Re-roll any offcuts with the remaining dough and roll out two triangles, each 22x22x18.5cm, for the front and back walls of the house. Into the front of the house, cut out two windows using the heart and circle cutters. With a knife, cut out a door hole, about 5.5cm high and 3cm wide. Cut out two doors, each about 7x2.5cm. Cut out a square base, 26x26cm. I moulded a chimney about 4.5x2cm but every house is different; this is simply a guide.

Rest in the fridge or a cool place for about half an hour. Preheat the oven to 180°C/fan 170°C/350°F/gas mark 4. Bake in batches, or all together if you have room in your oven, for 15–20 minutes. Re-trim straight away, as the dough may have spread a bit, and re-cut the heart and round windows, if necessary.

continued…

TO ASSEMBLE AND DECORATE

To assemble, place the gingerbread base on to the drum, securing with a little royal icing. Place the royal icing into a piping bag, snip the end, and stick the roofs and walls on to the base. You can do this in stages, using small boxes or cake tins for support until the gingerbread cottage is firmly stuck together.

Using royal icing as 'glue', decorate the house with the sweets then, with the no. 1 nozzle, pipe on the window and door decorations. Sprinkle the hundreds and thousands all around for the grass. Cut the Curly Wurlys to form the fence and gate, and add the flowers, securing them all again with the royal icing.

TO DECORATE
250g white royal icing
assortment of sweets of your choice; I used:
200 Jazzies (for the roof); 45 small red sweets; 2 strips of thin red liquorice (each 22cm long); 1 small piece liquorice (for the chimney); 1 small piece of candyfloss (for the smoke); 1 tub hundreds and thousands; 5 Curly Wurlys (for the fence); 1 spray of sugar flowers

SPECIAL EQUIPMENT
30x30cm square cake drum
2 piping bags, one fitted with no. 1 nozzle

Russian Dolls
LIME AND VODKA SYRUP CAKE

FOR THE CAKE
100g unsalted butter, melted and
    cooled, plus more for the tin
250g self-raising flour, sifted
30g cornflour
pinch of salt
4 eggs, lightly beaten
300g golden caster sugar
finely grated zest and juice of
    1 lime
150g crème fraîche

FOR THE SYRUP
30g golden caster sugar
½ tbsp vodka
finely grated zest and juice of
    ½ lime

FOR THE BUTTERCREAM
100g unsalted butter, softened
100g icing sugar, sifted
finely grated zest of ½ lime
1 tbsp vodka, to taste

These are bound to delight and will keep for a few days once made. Although I am not sure my five sugar Russian dolls would actually fit inside each other, they are still enchanting and fun to make, most especially the painting. It can be as simple or detailed as artistic talent and time allows! If you would rather, you could always draw the designs on the dolls using edible pens.

TO BAKE
Preheat the oven to 160°C/fan 150°C/325°F/gas mark 3. Butter a 20cm square cake tin and line the base with baking parchment.

Sift the flour, cornflour and salt together and set aside. Using the whisk attachment of an electric mixer, or a bowl and electric whisk, beat together the eggs, sugar and lime zest until light and fluffy and slightly thickened (this may take a good five minutes). Very gently fold in the crème fraîche, then the flour mixture, the melted butter and lastly the lime juice.

Pour the cake batter into the prepared tin and bake for 50–60 minutes, or until a skewer emerges clean. Cool completely in the tin.

For the syrup, melt together the sugar, vodka and lime zest and juice in a small pan. Bring to a boil, then set aside to cool.

To make the buttercream, beat the butter until really pale and fluffy. Add the icing sugar and lime zest. Beat for at least five minutes until light and creamy, adding the vodka slowly towards the end.

TO DECORATE

Once the cake is completely cold, turn it out of the tin, remove the papers and chill for a few hours or overnight in the fridge. Cut out four doll templates from paper; mine were 10cm high, 8cm, 7cm and 6cm. (I made four cake dolls; only three are shown in the photo.) Turn the cake flat-side up and lay the templates over it. With a sharp knife, cut out each body. Sculpt each one to shape, brush very lightly with the vodka syrup, then cover with a thin layer of the buttercream. Stand up each doll on the cut-out discs from the thin cake board – largest doll on the largest card – adhering with a little buttercream.

To cover each doll with sugarpaste, roll out a circle of sugarpaste 7mm thick, large enough to cover her sides too. Lay the centre of the circle of paste over the doll's head, and ease over her body. Rub to shape and mould with your hands; the sugarpaste is very malleable. Repeat with each doll. Mould a tiny doll, about 3.5cm high, from sugarpaste alone.

To make the sugar bases, roll out the remaining sugarpaste to 1.5cm thick and cut out four circles: 7.5cm, 7cm, 6cm and 5.5cm. Indent them horizontally around the edge. Allow the dolls to dry overnight, so the sugarpaste becomes dry enough to paint.

Paint the lower half of the base black and the upper part red. Then, using a very fine brush, outline the design on each doll in black. Then paint each doll. The designs are usually all a little different and individual, so don't aim for perfection. It is probably best to start with the face first and, if it goes wrong, just turn the doll around and try again! Place each doll on its base, sticking it on with edible glue.

✶ ALSO TRY WITH All-in-one Chocolate cake (see page 77), or Easiest Ever All-in-one Fruit Cake (see page 186)

TO DECORATE

1.3kg white sugarpaste
selection of food colour pastes:
    I used black; Christmas red;
    baby blue; claret; Christmas
    green; mint green; melon
edible glue

SPECIAL EQUIPMENT

15cm round thin cake board,
    cut into 4 circles: 5.5cm; 5cm;
    4.5cm; 3.5cm
set of round cutters
fine paint brushes

Black Forest Bombe
CHOCOLATE KIRSCH CAKE

SERVES 12

TO BAKE

Preheat the oven to 170°C/fan 160°C/340°F/gas mark 3½. Lightly butter two 20cm round tins and line the bases with baking parchment. Sift together the flour and baking powder, then stir in the almonds. Set a large bowl over a saucepan of barely simmering water, ensuring the bowl does not touch the water, and melt the chocolate, butter and 1 tbsp of water. Remove from the heat and beat in the sugar. Beat in the egg yolks, a couple at a time, then the Kirsch. Fold in the flour mixture. In a clean bowl, whisk the egg whites with the salt until soft peaks form. Take a big spoonful and fold it into the chocolate mixture to loosen, then fold in the rest. Divide between the tins, smooth the tops and bake for 18–20 minutes, or until a skewer emerges clean. Leave for a few minutes in the tin, then turn out on to a wire rack. Remove the papers. When cold, chill for a few hours to firm up.

Lightly whip the cream, the sugar and half the Kirsch to make the cream filling. Mix the remaining Kirsch with a spoonful or so of the morello syrup. Split both cakes in half horizontally. Line a 1.8-litre pudding basin with cling film. Find a round cutter the size of the base of the bowl and cut a circle of cake to line the base. Now cut strips to line the sides. Cut a circle to fit the middle. Leave one of the layers whole to fit the top. Sprinkle the cut cake with the syrup mixture.

TO ASSEMBLE AND DECORATE

Next, assemble the cake layer by layer, squidging it down to fill in any gaps, and using all the trimmings. Spread cream over the base circle, followed by a layer of half the morellos. Place on the middle disc of cake, another layer of cream, the remaining morellos, and the final layer of the cake. Cover with cling film, place a weight on top and chill overnight. To unmould, pull on the cling film and ease it out of the bowl. Place on the cake board, then on to a wire rack, with baking parchment underneath to catch the drips.

Melt the chocolate and cream in a bowl set over barely simmering water (make sure the bowl does not touch the water). Stir until smooth. If it is runny, let it cool to thicken. Pour over the cake, and allow to set for a few hours. Decorate with fresh cherries. You can entirely cover your bombe with cherries if you wish, sticking them on with cocktail sticks.

✱ ALSO TRY WITH Flourless Sachertorte (see page 70)

FOR THE CAKE
125g unsalted butter, plus more
    for the tins
50g plain flour
1 tsp baking powder
50g ground almonds
200g 70% cocoa solids chocolate
130g light muscovado sugar
4 eggs, separated
1 tbsp Kirsch
¼ tsp salt

FOR THE FILLING
400ml double cream
2 tbsp golden caster sugar
2 tbsp Kirsch
425g can of morello cherries,
    dried well; reserve the syrup

TO DECORATE
200g 70% cocoa solids chocolate
275ml double cream
a handful to 2 punnets of fresh
    cherries, to taste

SPECIAL EQUIPMENT
20cm round cake board

Chocolate, cherries and cream are a perfect combination and, if you use the very best ingredients, you will produce a delicious cake. If you don't wish to make the bombe, simply keep the two 20cm chocolate cakes as they are, split each in two and layer with cream and cherries.

Vampire
Party

Vampire Cupcakes
DEVIL'S CARDAMOM-CHOCOLATE CAKE

MAKES 12

FOR THE CAKES
12 cupcake cases
10 cardamom pods (optional)
50g plain flour
½ tsp baking powder
75g ground almonds
200g 70% cocoa solids chocolate, chopped
125g unsalted butter
130g light muscovado sugar
4 eggs, separated
1 tbsp brandy
¼ tsp salt

FOR THE FROSTING
180g white caster sugar
1 egg white
½ tsp cream of tartar
pinch of salt

FOR THE BLACK AND RED ROSES
160g white sugarpaste
claret food colour paste
Christmas red food colour paste
black food colour paste

FOR THE VAMPIRE BITES
1 tsp raspberry jam

Cakes fit for any vampire's party; he's even laid his fangs into some of them!

TO BAKE
Preheat the oven to 170°C/fan 160°C/340°F/gas mark 3½. Place the cupcake cases into a cupcake tin.

Deseed the cardamom pods, if using: split with a knife, empty out the seeds and grind to a powder in a mortar and pestle. Sift together the flour, baking powder and cardamom and stir in the ground almonds.

Set a large bowl over a saucepan of barely simmering water (make sure the bowl does not touch the water) and melt the chocolate, butter and 1 tbsp water. Once melted, remove from the heat and beat in the sugar. Beat the egg yolks into the mixture, a couple at a time, then add the brandy. Fold in the flour mixture and mix lightly together.

In a clean bowl, whisk the egg whites with the salt until soft peaks form. Take a big spoonful and fold into the chocolate mixture to loosen, then fold in the rest. Divide the batter between the cupcake cases and bake for 15–20 minutes, or until they spring back to the touch. Remove to cool on a wire rack.

TO DECORATE
To make the frosting, place all the ingredients with 2 tbsp water in a heatproof bowl standing over a pan of very, very gently simmering water; it must not be boiling. Then, with an electric whisk (don't even think about doing this with a hand whisk!) whisk for seven to 10 minutes, or until the icing has increased in volume, is thick and shiny and forms soft peaks. Working quickly as it will start to set, spread over the cupcakes, swirling with a small palette or kitchen knife.

To make the roses, colour 80g of sugarpaste red, using claret and Christmas red food colours, and 80g black (see page 168). Mould four roses from each colour (see page 121). Place one black or red rose on to each of eight cupcakes.

To make the fang marks, simply indent the icing of the four remaining cakes with a skewer, or the end of a teaspoon, and pour in a small amount of raspberry jam, allowing it to ooze over the frosting a little.

✱ ALSO TRY WITH Liquorice Toffee Cupcakes (see page 160)

Black Biscuits
CHOCOLATE SHORTBREAD

This recipe not only tastes delicious but is excellent for cutting, as it keeps its shape so well when baked.

TO BAKE
Sift the flour, salt, cocoa and icing sugar into a bowl. Rub in the butter with your fingers until well combined. Knead just until smooth but do not over-mix, or you will toughen the dough. Wrap in cling film and chill for about 30 minutes.

Lightly dust a clean board and rolling pin with flour, and roll out the dough to about 5mm thick. Cut out 20 bats and 20 hearts, using the larger heart cutter. Press two dragees into each bat for the eyes. Lay all the biscuits on a baking tray and chill for about 30 minutes. Preheat the oven to 170°C/fan 160°C/340°F/gas mark 3½. Bake for 10–12 minutes. Leave on the trays until cool.

TO DECORATE
For the hearts, mix the sugarpaste with claret food colour (see page 168). Lightly dust a work top with icing sugar and roll out the sugarpaste to about 2mm thick. Cut out 20 hearts with the smaller heart cutter. Sprinkle a little icing sugar over the heart biscuits and flick over a tiny amount of water – you don't want soggy biscuits – to create a glue. (Or brush the biscuits, three or four at a time, with edible glue.) Press the sugarpaste hearts on to the biscuits.

To decorate the bats, simply rub a little glitter over each biscuit with your fingers.

✱ ALSO TRY WITH Vanilla Shortbread (see page 186)

MAKES 20 BATS AND 20 BLEEDING
   HEARTS

250g plain flour, plus more
   to dust
½ tsp salt
50g cocoa powder
100g icing sugar
250g unsalted butter, softened
   and diced

TO DECORATE
40 small silver dragees
150g white sugarpaste
claret food colour paste
icing sugar, to dust
edible glue (optional)
edible clear glitter

SPECIAL EQUIPMENT
10cm bat cutter
5.5cm heart cutter
4.5cm heart cutter

The Crystal Skull

DEVIL'S CARDAMOM-CHOCOLATE CAKE

SERVES 8

FOR THE CAKE
unsalted butter, for the tins
1 x Devil's Cardamom-Chocolate
    Cake batter (see page 26)

FOR THE CHOCOLATE GANACHE
150g 70% cocoa solids chocolate,
    chopped
200ml double cream

SPECIAL EQUIPMENT
skull template (see opposite)
2 thin cake boards

For full-on bling, this cake is encrusted with more than 530 Swarovski crystals! Though you can always use dragees for a more economical option. The skull can be made weeks in advance, stored in a cardboard box, then placed on the cake on the day. If you double the cake and ganache recipes and bake for 35–45 minutes in a 30cm, 7.5cm deep round tin, this will make one large and delicious plain cake that you can decorate with gold leaf.

TO BAKE
Preheat the oven to 170°C/fan 160°C/340°F/gas mark 3½. Lightly butter two 20cm round cake tins and line the bases with baking parchment. Divide the batter between the tins and bake for 18–20 minutes, or until a skewer emerges clean. Remove from the oven. Leave for a few minutes in the tin, then turn out on to a wire rack and remove the papers.

When the cakes are completely cold, trim the top surfaces flat, if necessary, and place them in the fridge to firm up. (They can be made in advance and freeze well.)

TO SHAPE AND COVER THE CAKE
Now, draw or trace a skull, complete with all the facial markings. It needs to be 20cm long to completely cover the cake. Trace its outline on to both cake boards, then cut out the shapes with a sharp pair of scissors or a knife. Reserve the original skull drawing. Place one of the boards on top of each cake in turn and cut around using a sharp knife.

To make the ganache, melt together the chocolate and cream in a heatproof bowl over barely simmering water. Make sure the bowl does not touch the water. Stir until smooth. If it is very runny, let it cool to thicken. Spread a thin layer between the two cakes, and sandwich them together. Stand the cake on one of the skull-shaped boards, using a little ganache to attach it, and place on a wire rack, with baking parchment underneath to catch the drips. Pour over the ganache. Allow to harden for a few hours before adding the skull.

TO DECORATE

Take about 50g white sugarpaste and colour it black using the food colour (see page 168). Seal in a polythene bag and set aside. Brush the second skull-shaped cake board with a little edible glue.

Take about half the remaining sugarpaste and mould into a rough oval to completely cover the board, making it thicker at the top (for the forehead) and tapering towards the chin. Smooth all the edges with your fingers (none of the board should be showing). Press in your thumbs, to form the two eye sockets and the nose.

To make the mouth, cut out a template using your original skull drawing and mark with a knife. Remove excess sugarpaste to create the mouth void and line with the black sugarpaste. Roll two thin sausages from the black sugarpaste and place them behind where the teeth will be at the top and bottom, to support the teeth. Make teeth 'sockets' by indenting the sugarpaste around the mouth with the end of the paint brush.

Use most of the remaining white sugarpaste to build up the forehead, bridge of the nose, the cheekbones and the top of the mouth. Mould and smooth the icing with your fingers. Don't worry about all the seams of icing, they will be covered up by the crystals, you just need to be satisfied with the overall shape. Seal the remaining sugarpaste in a polythene bag and set aside. Lay the skull on to a protected surface and spray with the pearl lustre spray. Leave for a few hours to dry.

To apply the crystals, paint about 5cm square of the skull at a time with edible glue, then position the smaller crystals with the tweezers. I found it easiest to start in the middle of the skull and work outwards, outlining the mouth, eyes and nose areas first. The two sides need to be more or less symmetrical. Use the two large crystals to form a medallion at the centre of the forehead.

To make the teeth, take small pieces of the remaining white sugarpaste and form into teeth shapes with your fingers. When you are happy with the teeth, place them into the tooth sockets, top and bottom, sticking with edible glue. Stick the tiny dragee on one of the top teeth. Place the skull on top of the chocolate cake.

✱ ALSO TRY WITH Flourless Sachertorte (see page70), or All-in-one Chocolate Cake (see page 77), or Madeira Cake (see page 99)

TO DECORATE
500g white sugarpaste
black food colour paste
edible glue

SPECIAL EQUIPMENT
small paint brush
1 can edible pearl lustre spray
2 packets Swarovski 6mm non-hot fix clear crystals (see page 188 for crystal supplier)
tweezers
1 x 16mm non-hot fix Rivoli round clear crystal
1 x 18x10.5mm sew-on stone clear crystal
1 tiny dragee

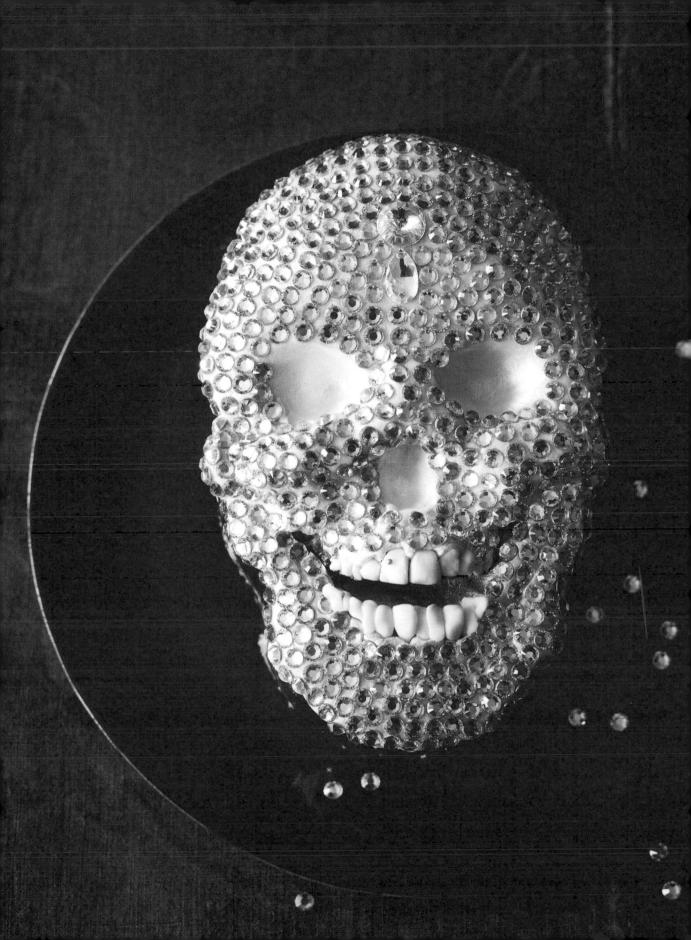

Bridge Traybake
COFFEE CAKE

SERVES 12

FOR THE CAKE
1 x Tiramisu Cake (see page 155),
    baked in a 20cm square cake
    tin for 35–40 minutes

FOR THE SYRUP
3 tbsp very strong black coffee
    (espresso or instant), cooled
3 tbsp Tia Maria, dark rum
    or Kahlua

FOR THE COFFEE BUTTERCREAM
250g unsalted butter, softened
250g icing sugar, sifted
2 tbsp very strong coffee

SPECIAL EQUIPMENT
1 set tiny aspic cutters

TO DECORATE
icing sugar, to dust
600g white sugarpaste
black food colour paste
red food colour paste
edible clear glitter (optional)
20g bag white royal icing

Play your winning hand and produce this for any keen bridge player. Of course any 20cm square cake can be used. The tiny hearts, diamonds, spades and clubs can be made weeks beforehand and stored in a cardboard box ready to decorate on the day.

TO BAKE
When the cake is baked and cooled, trim the top flat, turn it upside down and slice in half. Mix the coffee and liqueur for the syrup and sprinkle it over both cakes. Place the base cake (the one that was baked on top) baked-side down on a serving plate or cake stand.

For the buttercream, cream the butter and icing sugar together for three to five minutes, or until light and fluffy, then very slowly beat in the coffee. Spread half the buttercream on the base layer and half on the top, then sandwich together.

TO DECORATE
On a clean work surface lightly dusted with icing sugar, roll out 500g of the white sugarpaste into a rough square slightly larger than 20cm and 4mm thick. Trim to 20cm square with a large knife (using the baking tin as a guide) and lift on to the cake. Trim the edges if necessary. With a ruler, mark out four cards across and three cards down on the edges of the sugarpaste; each card measures 5x6.5cm. Lay the blade of a large knife right across the middle to make the central vertical line first. Mark the other lines in the same way. You will have 12 more or less equal playing cards.

Take the remaining 100g white sugarpaste and divide in half. Using the food colour pastes, colour 50g black and the other 50g red (see page 168). On a clean work surface lightly dusted with icing sugar, roll out the black sugarpaste quite thinly (about 2mm thick). Cut out about 10 clubs and 12 spades with the aspic cutters. Roll out the red sugarpaste, sprinkle with the glitter, if using, then press down lightly with the rolling pin; it will stick very well. Cut out about nine hearts and 20 diamonds.

Let the decorations dry for at least an hour or so, then, using the royal icing, attach to the playing cards. Cut the cake to serve.

✶ ALSO TRY WITH Flourless Sachertorte (see page 70), or Honey Cake (see page 183), or Toffee Cake (see page 187)

Turkish Delight Meringue

The exotic flavours of rose water and pistachio both appear in this delicious meringue filled with raspberry jelly. Make the jelly and meringue the day before, then whip the cream and assemble shortly before serving.

To make the jelly, soak the gelatine in a bowl of cold water for about 10 minutes. In a saucepan, place 400g of the raspberries, the lemon juice and sugar. Simmer over a very, very gentle heat for 10–15 minutes; you will see the juices come from the raspberries. Pour into a sieve set over a bowl and allow the juice to drip through, trying not to press the fruit if you want a clear jelly. While the juice is still hot, squeeze the gelatine leaves hard to remove the excess water and add to the raspberry juices. Stir to dissolve, add the remaining raspberries and the rose water, cover and leave to set overnight in the fridge.

To make the meringue, preheat the oven to 210°C/fan 200°C/410°F/ gas mark 6½. Cut two 23cm circles from baking parchment and place on two separate baking trays. Put the egg whites into a degreased bowl (rubbed with a cut lemon and wiped dry with kitchen towel). Add all the icing sugar. Whisk the egg whites and sugar until soft peaks form and the mixture is marshmallowy. This may take up to 10 minutes, so you'll need an electric whisk!

Spread on to the two circles with a spatula and sprinkle with the pistachio nuts. Reduce the oven now to the lowest you can (mine was 80°C/fan 70°C/175°F/gas mark ¼). Bake for 1¾–2 hours, or until dry and crispy on the outside and probably a bit cracked; this is absolutely fine. Turn off the oven and leave the meringues in there until completely cold. If you have made this the evening before, leave overnight in the oven. Remove the papers.

Whip the cream until thickened, adding the rose water and most of the icing sugar, to taste. This meringue won't keep very well, so assemble only a few hours before serving. Place one meringue on a serving plate, spread with all the cream, then spoon over a layer of raspberry jelly. Place the other meringue on top. Finish with a dusting of icing sugar.

SERVES 8

FOR THE RASPBERRY JELLY
2 leaves (4g) gelatine
600g raspberries
juice of ½ lemon
100g caster sugar
1–1½ tbsp rose water (to taste; do take care, taste as you add)

FOR THE ALL-IN-ONE MERINGUE
6 egg whites
350g golden (or white) icing sugar, sifted
50g unsalted pistachio nuts, chopped

FOR THE CREAM
300ml double cream
1–2 tsp rose water (to taste; do take care, taste as you add)
1–2 tbsp icing sugar, plus more to dust

Strawberry and Elderflower Cake

SERVES 24 (HALVE THE RECIPE TO
SERVE 12)

FOR THE CAKE
450g unsalted butter, really soft,
  diced, plus more for the tins
450g self-raising flour
2 tsp baking powder
8 eggs, lightly beaten
finely grated zest of 2 large
  unwaxed lemons
450g golden caster sugar
4 tbsp elderflower cordial

FOR THE ELDERFLOWER CREAM
1.2kg ripe, even-sized
  strawberries, cleaned, dried
  and hulled
2 tbsp golden caster sugar
1 tsp vanilla extract
600ml double cream
8 tbsp elderflower cordial

As I write, the hedgerows are filled with creamy, lacy elderflower heads, crying out to be turned into a fragrant cordial. Elderflowers have an extraordinary affinity with strawberries, and make a perfect summer cake. Assemble only a couple of hours before the event (and chill, if you can) as the cake won't keep, especially in the heat. A summer celebration on a plate!

TO BAKE

Preheat the oven to 180°C/fan 170°C/350°F/gas mark 4. To make the three-tiered cake, take three 20cm round sandwich tins. Butter the tins and line the bases with baking parchment. If you have only two tins, then make the cake mixture and divide it evenly into three batches, baking the third as soon as a tin becomes free.

For this cake, I use an electric mixer and beater attachment, but you can use a food processor, or a bowl and electric whisk, if you prefer. Sift the flour and baking powder into the bowl, add the butter, eggs, lemon zest and sugar, and beat well, adding the cordial towards the end. Be careful not to over-mix, as you want a light cake.

Bake for 30–35 minutes, or until a skewer emerges clean. (To halve the recipe, bake in two 20cm tins for 20–25 minutes.) Remove from the oven, leave for a couple of minutes, run a knife around the rim to loosen the cakes from the tins and turn out on to a wire rack. Remove the papers and leave to cool completely. Trim the cakes flat.

FOR THE FILLING AND DECORATION

Slice 400g of the strawberries and toss in a bowl with the sugar and vanilla. Leave all the flavours to mingle together for 30 minutes.

Whip the cream until soft peaks form, adding the cordial slowly just as it begins to thicken. Place one cake on a cake stand and spread with a layer of cream and half the sliced strawberries. Repeat with another cake, a layer of cream and the remaining sliced strawberries. Top with the last cake. Spread the remaining cream all over the top and sides.

Take the best-shaped 20 strawberries and cut 10–12 in half. Place the halved strawberries, cut side up, in a circle around the edge of the cake, and pile up the rest in the centre. Cut the remaining strawberries into slices – or in half – and press into the cream all around the sides.

ELDERFLOWER CORDIAL

MAKES ABOUT 1.3 LITRES

I have been making this for many years, it is so superior to anything you can buy. Citric acid can be a little hard to come by (the supply is restricted as it is also used by drug addicts) but you should be able to find it at the chemist. To check elderflowers are in their prime, shake them; the little flowers should stay on the branches.

Shake the elderflowers to dislodge any resident insects and remove the larger stems, as they will affect the flavour. Bring 1 litre of water to a boil, add the sugar and stir to ensure it is all dissolved. Cool for about 15 minutes, then add the elderflowers, citric acid and lemons, give it a good stir, cover and leave for 24 hours for the flavours to mingle.

Dampen either a sheet of muslin, a clean J-cloth or a tea towel with boiling water, wring dry and use it to line a sieve. If you are keeping the cordial for a month or two, you will need to sterilise some glass screw-topped bottles: rinse them out thoroughly, then place them upside down in the dishwasher and run a full cycle. Or preheat the oven to 140°C/fan 130°C/275°F/gas mark 1. Stand the clean, empty bottles (without lids) in the oven for 15 minutes. Remove, allow to cool, then strain the cordial into the bottles. Store in the fridge.

20 fresh elderflower heads
600g granulated or caster sugar
25g citric acid
3 large unwaxed lemons, sliced

strawberry and elderflower cake   39

Playing Dice

BANOFFEE CAKE

FOR THE CAKE
120g unsalted butter, softened,
  plus more for the tins
250g self-raising flour
1 tsp baking powder
pinch of salt
¼ tsp ground nutmeg
1 tsp ground cinnamon
160g light muscovado sugar
3 extremely ripe, large bananas
  (or 4 small); they should be
  brown, not yellow
2 eggs, lightly beaten
1 tsp vanilla extract
2 tbsp whole milk

FOR THE TOFFEE BUTTERCREAM
240g unsalted butter, softened
60g light muscovado sugar
2 tbsp golden syrup
1 tbsp double cream
1 tsp vanilla extract
200g icing sugar, sifted

May lady luck smile down on the special someone that gets to eat these giant edible dice! To make the two dice shown in the picture you will need to double all the ingredients.

TO BAKE
Preheat the oven to 180°C/fan 170°C/350°F/gas mark 4. Butter two deep 13cm square cake tins and line the bases with baking parchment. If your tins are not deep, make a collar of a double thickness of baking parchment to come up above their sides.

Sift together the flour, baking powder, salt, nutmeg and cinnamon.

Cream together the butter and sugar, using an electric whisk or in an electric mixer, until light and fluffy (this may take five minutes). Meanwhile, mash the bananas with a fork. Add the eggs, vanilla and milk to the butter mixture, then a spoonful of flour. Fold in the remaining flour mixture, then the bananas, and pour the batter into the tins. Bake for 40 minutes, or until a skewer emerges clean. Remove from the oven, run a knife around the tin and leave for a few minutes. Turn out on to a wire rack, remove the papers, and cool completely.

For the toffee buttercream, simmer 80g of the butter, the muscovado sugar and syrup over a low heat in a pan until it is a deep caramel colour. Remove from the heat and add the cream and vanilla extract. Keep stirring. Allow to cool.

In an electric mixer, beat the remaining butter until really pale and fluffy, add the icing sugar and beat for at least five minutes, or until light and creamy. Add all the cooled toffee mixture and beat in well.

TO DECORATE

Trim the two cakes so they are level. Split each cake in half horizontally. Spread a little toffee buttercream on to the board and place one of the cakes on to it. Repeat to make four layers, making sure the flat base of a cake is uppermost. Spread the remaining buttercream over the top and sides of the cake and the board.

On a work surface lightly dusted with icing sugar, roll out the white sugarpaste to a 35cm square about 5mm thick. Roll loosely around the rolling pin and place over the cake. Smooth the icing all over the cake – covering the edges of the board too – and rub with your hands. Cut away any excess from the edges. Leave to harden for an hour or so.

Meanwhile, on a work surface lightly dusted with icing sugar, roll out the black sugarpaste to about 2mm thick. Using the round cutter, cut out about 20 dots. Using the edible glue or royal icing, attach to the die, each side with a different number of dots. To be extra realistic remember that, on a real die, the number of dots on opposing sides add up to seven.

✱ ALSO TRY WITH Masala Chai Cake (see page 184), baked for 40 minutes at 170°C/fan 160°C/340°F/gas mark 3½

TO DECORATE
icing sugar, to dust
1kg white sugarpaste
    (or red, for a red die)
100g black sugarpaste
    (or white sugarpaste and
    black food colour paste)
edible glue, or 20g bag white
    royal icing

SPECIAL EQUIPMENT
13cm cake board
3cm round cutter

Jewel Box
AUSTRALIAN PANFORTE

Based on an old Australian recipe, this cake is simplicity itself to make and is packed with whole nuts and fruits, bound with a little butterless cake batter. If you prefer, you could make a more tasteful, reserved cake using dark, undyed cherries.

Preheat the oven to 140°C/fan 130°C/275°F/gas mark 1. Butter a 20cm, 7.5cm deep square cake tin and line the base with baking parchment. Wrap with a collar of brown paper tied with string.

Roast the whole nuts on a baking tray for about 10 minutes. If necessary, rinse the cherries of excess syrup: place in a sieve and run under warm water. Dry carefully with kitchen paper.

Sift the flour and salt into a bowl, and stir in the sugar. Tip all the whole fruits and candied peel into a large mixing bowl, add the whole nuts, lemon zest and ginger. Beat in the eggs and vanilla and add the flour mixture. Tip the batter into the prepared tin. Make a graphic pattern with the halved cherries all over the top. Bake for 1½–2 hours, or until a skewer emerges clean.

Remove from the oven and leave the cake to cool in the tin on a wire rack. When cool, prick with a skewer between the cherries and spoon over the rum. Carefully remove from the tin, remove the papers and place on the cake board. Gently warm the apricot jam, press it through a sieve if necessary, mix with the lemon juice and brush all over the cherries to glaze. Add the bejewelled ribbon to the sides of the cake. It will keep for a week or so wrapped in foil in an airtight tin. Feed occasionally with a little more rum, if you wish.

SERVES 25

FOR THE CAKE
unsalted butter, for the tin
180g whole brazil nuts
180g whole pecan nuts
180g multi-coloured glacé cherries
100g self-raising flour
1 tsp salt
140g golden caster sugar
250g dates, stoned but whole
50g raisins, Lexia if possible
100g large pieces of candied peel, roughly chopped (not pre-chopped in little packets!)
finely grated zest of 1 unwaxed lemon
50g crystallised stem ginger, roughly chopped
3 eggs, lightly beaten
1 tsp vanilla extract
3 tbsp dark rum or brandy, or to taste, plus more to feed (optional)

TO DECORATE
350g multi-coloured glacé cherries, halved
3 tbsp apricot jam
squeeze of lemon juice

SPECIAL EQUIPMENT
25cm square cake board
80cm (4cm-wide) bejewelled ribbon

Robots
CRISPY MARS BAR FRIDGE CAKE

These friendly robots will delight any young child, both to help create and as a party centrepiece. Make several batches and assemble an army!

Butter a 23cm square loose-bottomed cake tin, and line the base with baking parchment. Tip the rice cereal into a large mixing bowl.

Melt the Mars Bars, chocolate, butter and syrup in a bowl over gently simmering water, making sure the bowl does not touch the water and stirring from time to time. Once the mixture has melted, tip it into the rice cereal and stir well until combined. Pour into the prepared tin, and press down with the back of a spoon or a palette knife to make it compact. Place in the fridge to set for at least a couple of hours, or preferably overnight.

When ready to make the robots, tip out the square on to a chopping board. You must cut out the heads and bodies first, then the legs and arms. The feet and necks can then be cut out from what's left. Once you have cut out your robots, assemble the bodies with cocktail sticks.

Place the two different types of melted chocolate into two piping bags and decorate the robots as you wish, sticking on sweets and dragees as you do so.

MAKES 2 ROBOTS (SERVES 12–15)

FOR THE ROBOTS
100g unsalted butter, diced, plus more for the tin
200g crispy puffed rice cereal
4 Mars Bars (total weight 240g), roughly chopped
350g 55% cocoa solids chocolate, chopped
1 tbsp golden syrup

TO DECORATE
100g white chocolate, melted
100g 55% cocoa solids chocolate, melted
an assortment of silver and coloured chocolate beans, and silver dragees in several sizes

TO CONSTRUCT

For one robot you will need:
- 1 HEAD 7x7cm
- 1 NECK 2.5x1.5cm
- 1 BODY 8.5x8.5cm
- 2 ARMS 8.5x2.5cm
- 2 LEGS 5x2.5cm
- 2 FEET 3.5x2.5cm

Vintage
Tea Party

Crocodile Handbag

MADEIRA CAKE

The day before you decorate the bag, colour all the sugarpaste with the claret food colour to make a burgundy shade (see page 168). If you try to do this on the day, because you are adding so much colour you may struggle to roll it out. Also, colour the modelling paste for the handles the same colour. Roll it into a sausage, about 30x10cm, and bend into a 'U' shape with a 7cm gap between the ends. Leave overnight, or longer if possible, to dry out thoroughly.

As always, put the cakes in the fridge or freezer for an hour or so to firm up before you mould them. Cut the cake board to size (about 20x9cm) and cut a 'V' in the two shorter ends (the indent of the two sides of the cake).

On a clean work surface, lay the two cakes out in front of you. Trim the surfaces so they are level and, with a serrated or sharp knife, cut a slice from both cakes so they each measure 20x15cm. Sandwich together the two cut surfaces with the buttercream, spreading well to the edges. Carve the top length of the cake so that it is rounded and slightly narrower at the top than the bottom (which is the base of the bag). Spread buttercream all over the surface of the board and stand the cake upright on to it. Trim the bottom side edges to fit, cutting two 'V' shapes into the cake at the sides. You may need to return the cake to the fridge for half an hour to firm up if it becomes crumbly.

Spread the remaining buttercream all over every surface of the cake. Cut the dowelling into three and insert in a row through the centre, about 5cm apart, to help support the cake.

Dust the work top with icing sugar and knead about two-thirds of the sugarpaste. Roll out to a 5mm thick rectangle, about 25x30cm long. Keep running a palette knife underneath to stop it from sticking to the work top. Press the cobblestone mat quite firmly on to the sugarpaste. If the sugarpaste is too sticky, you may need a fine dusting of icing sugar on the mat. It is best to practice with the mat first if it is unfamiliar, to work out how much pressure you need. The mat is slightly smaller than the rolled-out sugarpaste, but is the perfect size to cover the cake as it will slightly stretch as you lift it with your hands. Lift the sugarpaste on to the cake and very, very gently ease it into position over the front, top and back. Remember, the part most visible is the front, and the top will be covered by the flap.

SERVES 20

FOR THE CAKE AND TO DECORATE
1kg white sugarpaste
claret food colour paste
50g Mexican modelling paste
   (see suppliers, page 188)
2 x 20cm square Madeira Cakes
   brushed with lemon syrup
   (see page 99)
1 x Lemon Buttercream recipe,
   softened (see page 99)
icing sugar, to dust
60g bag burgundy-coloured royal
   icing, no. 1 nozzle
edible glaze spray (optional)
2mm and 4mm gold dragees

SPECIAL EQUIPMENT
20cm square cake board
30cm white dowelling rod
1 cobblestone mat (see suppliers,
   page 188)
3cm heart cutter
tweezers (optional)

continued...

My fantasy cake! I've made a burgundy crocodile bag, but make any bag of your choice. A Mulberry maybe, or a Louis Vuitton; you'll save your pennies and there's no waiting list. Remember: the more food colour in the sugarpaste, the harder it will be to use.

Trim all the edges very carefully... you may find a sharp pair of scissors is a lot easier than a knife here! Do keep any clean, buttercream-free sugarpaste to re-roll, sealed in a polythene bag. If for any reason the cake needs support as it dries, place something heavy behind it to stop it tipping.

Next you need to cut sugarpaste for the sides of the bag. Roll out a rectangle about the same length as the textured mat (28cm) and 12cm wide. Press the mat on to the sugarpaste and cut it into two 13x9cm pieces. Mould with your fingers to fit, shaping the slight dent either side and the 'V' at the base, trying not to lose the crocodile finish as you do so. Join up to the edges of the central part of sugarpaste as neatly as you can. Roll thin sausages of sugarpaste and glue with royal icing to the seams where the front and sides meet.

Now make the handbag flap, by rolling out a piece of sugarpaste about 25x17–18cm, rounding the edges. Indent with the mat. When you are happy with the shape, pipe a little royal icing on to the top surface of the cake, lift the flap on to the cake and position and trim to size; it extends about 5cm down the back. With a cocktail stick, indent tiny stitch holes all around the edges of the flap. Indent two holes at the top of the flap with a wooden spoon handle or similar, 7cm apart, for the handle. Fill the holes with royal icing, and insert the handle. Spray the entire cake with the glaze, if using, and allow to dry.

To make the heart decoration, simply roll out a small piece of sugarpaste on a clean board lightly dusted with icing sugar to about 3mm thick. Using the heart cutter, cut out one heart. Stick on the dragees with the royal icing. I placed the larger ones around the edge and the small ones in the centre, a pair of tweezers will help. When dry, attach the heart to the centre of the handbag flap.

✶ ALSO TRY WITH All-in-one Chocolate Cake (see page 77), or Honey Cake (see page 183), or Easiest Ever All-in-one Fruit Cake (see page 186)

Earl Grey Tea Fairy Cakes

MAKES 24 SMALL FAIRY CAKES

FOR THE FAIRY CAKES
15 fairy cake paper cases
200ml whole milk
3 Earl Grey tea bags
100g raisins (Lexia or Muscat
    if possible)
10 crushed cardamom pods
240g self-raising flour
1 tsp baking powder
140g unsalted butter, softened
100g golden caster sugar
finely grated zest of 1 orange
2 eggs, lightly beaten

FOR THE LEMON BUTTERCREAM
200g unsalted butter, softened
finely grated zest and juice of
    2 unwaxed lemons
300g icing sugar, sifted

TO DECORATE
a few blueberries, raspberries or
    blackberries
selection of small edible
    flowers, such as pansies,
    violas, rosebuds, rose petals
    or sweet geranium leaves

When I started my business around the kitchen table all those years ago, there was always a pot of Earl Grey tea on the go while we listened to Radio 4 as we worked! How things have changed... I have made these cakes with Earl Grey tea, but do make them with your favourite blend. Perfect for an afternoon tea party.

TO BAKE
Preheat the oven to 170°C/fan 160°C/340°F/gas mark 3½. Place the paper cases into two fairy cake tins.

Heat the milk in a saucepan until it comes to a boil. Remove the pan from the heat, add the tea bags, raisins and crushed cardamom pods. Cover and leave for an hour or so at room temperature for all the delicious flavours to mingle together. Taste the milk, which should be really flavourful. Strain the milk, squeezing the milk from the tea bags. Squeeze the milk from the raisins and set aside separately. Discard the cardamom pods.

In a bowl, sift the flour and baking powder together. Cream the butter, sugar and orange zest for about five minutes until light and fluffy. Add the eggs slowly, adding a spoonful of flour if necessary to stop the mixture from curdling. Next mix in the Earl Grey milk in two batches. Fold in the remaining flour and lastly the raisins.

Divide the batter between the cases and bake for 15–20 minutes, or until the cakes spring back to the touch. Remove from the oven and leave in the tins for a minute or two, then cool on a wire rack.

To make the buttercream, in an electric mixer, or with a hand-held electric whisk, beat the butter until really pale and fluffy. Add the lemon zest and icing sugar and continue to beat for about another five minutes until light and fluffy. Add the lemon juice gradually and keep beating, tasting as you add it. You may not need all the juice.

TO DECORATE
To ice the cakes, spread the buttercream on to the little cakes and decorate with your chosen berries and edible flowers. Serve with a pot of Earl Grey tea.

✱ ALSO TRY WITH Devil's Chocolate-Cardamom Cake (see page 26)

Tiny Rose and Violet Creams

TO BAKE

Preheat the oven to 170°C/fan 160°C/340°F/gas mark 3½. Butter a 20cm square cake tin and line the base with baking parchment. Sift the flour and baking powder together.

Place the chocolate in a bowl. Bring the milk to a boil and pour it over. Stir until the chocolate has melted, then cool to blood temperature.

Cream the butter and sugar together for a couple of minutes, then slowly beat in the eggs and vanilla extract, adding 1 tbsp flour to prevent curdling. Slowly add the cooled chocolate mixture, then fold in the sifted flour mixture and ground almonds.

Pour into the prepared tin and bake for about 25 minutes, or until a skewer emerges clean. Remove from the oven and leave to cool in the tin for a few minutes, then turn out on to a wire rack until cold. Place in the freezer for 30 minutes to firm up, so it will be easier to cut.

Divide the fondant between two bowls. To one, add a pinprick of pink food colour, and rose water to taste, to form a stiff dough. If it is too runny, knead in a little white icing sugar. The fondants need to be quite strong in flavour. Repeat with the other bowl, adding the violet liqueur and food colour until you have a stiff dough.

TO DECORATE

Split the cake in half horizontally and, using the cutter, cut 30 rounds from one layer of cake and 30 rounds from the other.

Lay the little circles of cake out on to a tray and divide the fondant equally between them: 30 balls of rose and 30 balls of violet. Chill in the fridge for one hour until the fondant has hardened. Meanwhile, melt the chocolate by placing it in a bowl over gently simmering water, making sure the bowl does not touch the water.

Lay out all the cakes on two wire racks (one flavour on each tray) with a sheet of baking parchment under each to catch the drips. Spoon over the chocolate, re-using any that drips through the racks. Decorate each cake with a crystallised rose or violet, as appropriate. They will keep for several days.

MAKES 60 (30 ROSE AND 30 VIOLET)

FOR THE CAKES
100g unsalted butter, softened, plus more for the tin
60g self-raising flour
1 tsp baking powder
100g 70% cocoa solids chocolate, finely chopped
80ml whole milk
120g dark muscovado sugar
2 eggs, lightly beaten
1 tsp vanilla extract
40g ground almonds

TO FILL AND DECORATE
500g bag fondant powder
pink food colour paste
4–5 tsp rose water
white icing sugar, if necessary
4–5 tsp violet liqueur
grape violet food colour paste
400g 70% cocoa solids chocolate, roughly chopped
30 crystallised rose petals
30 crystallised violet petals

SPECIAL EQUIPMENT
3cm round cutter

Reminiscent of lace gloves and nosegays from a more genteel era, and perfect served at the end of a special celebratory meal, or with afternoon tea. If you choose not to buy the violet liqueur, just make the rose cakes (you will need to double the quantities of rose fondant). Remember that different types of rose water and violet liqueur vary hugely in strength, so add little by little to taste.

Chewy, Gooey, Nutty Caramel Bars

I love these delicious bars and because they contain nuts, seeds and berries I can tell myself that they are relatively healthy! You can vary the nuts and berries; try any combination of hazelnuts, almonds, pecan nuts and dried cranberries or blueberries.

Preheat the oven to 170°C/fan 160°C/340°F/gas mark 3½. Lightly butter a 20cm square, loose-bottomed cake tin, and line the base with baking parchment.

Spread the pine nuts and pistachios out on a baking tray and lightly roast for four or five minutes. Remove from the oven and cool.

In a small pan, bring the butter, sugar and honey up to a boil and bubble away for two or three minutes, stirring all the while as it catches easily. Then add the cream and vanilla and cook for another minute or so. Set aside to cool down a little.

In a large bowl, mix all the nuts, coconut, oats, seeds and berries and pour in the caramel mixture. Mix well, then tip into the prepared tin. Bake in the oven for 12–15 minutes; it will darken a little, especially around the sides. Leave in the tin on a wire rack to cool. Chill in the fridge for an hour or so to firm up, then remove the papers and cut into 10 bars.

MAKES 10

135g unsalted butter, diced, plus more for the tin
45g pine nuts
90g unsalted pistachios, roughly chopped (not too small)
120g light muscovado sugar
2 tbsp runny honey
45ml double cream
½ tsp vanilla extract
100g desiccated coconut
60g rolled oats
50g sunflower seeds
45g sesame seeds
50g goji berries

Very Lemony Meringue Cake

ALL-IN-ONE LEMON CAKE

A true citrus hit, laced with a lemon syrup and with a creamy lemon curd filling. Of course, you can always omit the meringue for a simpler, equally delicious cake.

TO BAKE
To make the meringues, preheat the oven to 140°C/fan 130°C/275°F/ gas mark 1. Line a baking tray with baking parchment. Place the egg whites and icing sugar in a scrupulously clean and dry metal or glass bowl and, using an electric hand-held whisk, whisk until they form soft, shiny, marshmallowy peaks. This will take eight to 10 minutes. Drop tablespoons of the mixture on to the prepared tray and bake for 35–45 minutes. They are ready when they are crisp on the outside and sound hollow when tapped on the base. Remove from the oven and set aside to cool. They can be stored for a few days in an airtight tin.

Increase the oven temperature to 180°C/fan 170°C/350°F/gas mark 4. Butter two 20cm round sandwich tins and line the bases with baking parchment. For this batter, I use an electric mixer and beater attachment, but do use a food processor, or a bowl and an electric whisk, if you prefer.

Sift the flour and baking powder into the bowl, then add the lemon zest, sugar, butter and eggs. Beat together and lastly add the lemon juice. Do not over-mix.

Divide the batter between the two tins. Bake for 25–30 minutes, or until a skewer emerges clean. Meanwhile make the syrup by mixing the juice and sugar in a bowl. As soon as the cakes come from the oven, prick them all over with a cocktail stick and spoon over the syrup. Allow to cool in the tins on a wire rack. When cold, remove the papers. Trim each cake level, and split in half horizontally.

Mix the crème fraîche lightly with the lemon curd, so that it is marbled, not completely blended.

TO DECORATE
Place one of the cakes on to a plate or cake stand. Spread with some of the crème fraîche mixture, and repeat to make four layers. Spread the crème fraîche mixture all over the top and sides. Lightly press the almonds all around the sides. Place the meringues on top, you may not need them all. Finish with a sprinkling of lemon zest.

SERVES 8

FOR THE MERINGUES (MAKES 8–9)
2 egg whites, at room
    temperature
120g white icing sugar, sifted

FOR THE LEMON CAKE
250g unsalted butter, softened,
    diced, plus more for the tins
250g self-raising flour
1 tsp baking powder
finely grated zest of 2 large
    unwaxed lemons and juice of 1
250g golden caster sugar
4 large eggs, lightly beaten

FOR THE SYRUP
juice of 1 lemon
5 tbsp caster sugar

TO FILL AND DECORATE
300g crème fraîche (half-fat if
    preferred) or mascarpone
300g good lemon curd,
    preferably home made
100g flaked almonds, lightly
    toasted
finely grated zest of 1 unwaxed
    lemon

Flourless Lemon Polenta Cake

WITH LIMONCELLO SYRUP

SERVES 10

FOR THE CAKE
275g unsalted butter, softened,
    plus more for the tin
200g ground almonds
100g instant polenta
1 tsp baking powder
½ tsp salt
250g golden caster sugar
finely grated zest of 2 large
    unwaxed lemons and juice of 1
5 eggs, lightly beaten
2 tbsp limoncello

FOR THE CANDIED LEMONS
100g caster sugar
2 unwaxed lemons, very thinly
    sliced
2 tbsp limoncello

A rustic, very moist Italian cake to be enjoyed at any time, perhaps with a glass or two of limoncello…

Preheat the oven to 170°C/fan 160°C/340°F/gas mark 3½. Butter a 23cm, 7.5cm deep, round springform cake tin and line the base with baking parchment.

Place the ground almonds, polenta, baking powder and salt in a bowl.

In an electric mixer, or using a bowl and a hand-held whisk, cream together the butter, sugar and lemon zest until light and fluffy; this may well take five minutes. Add the eggs gradually, fold in the ground almond mixture and drizzle in the lemon juice and limoncello slowly at the end. Blend together well.

Pour the batter into the prepared tin and bake for 35–45 minutes, or until a skewer emerges clean. Leave in the tin, standing on a wire rack.

While the cake is baking, make the candied lemon slices by placing the caster sugar and 100ml water in a small pan. Dissolve all the sugar over a low heat, then increase the heat to medium and add the lemon slices. Simmer for about 10–15 minutes, stirring occasionally; do not allow to boil. The syrup will thicken.

As soon as the cakes come from the oven, prick them all over with a cocktail stick. Take 1 tbsp of the warm syrup, add the limoncello and spoon over the cake. Arrange the candied lemon slices over the top.

Eastern Tile Mosaic
FLOURLESS APRICOT-CARDAMOM CAKE

SERVES 12

FOR THE CAKE
unsalted butter, for the tin
20 green cardamom pods
225g drained weight (411g can)
    apricots in juice or syrup
    (reserve the liquid)
50g unsalted pistachio nuts
5 eggs, lightly beaten
200g golden caster sugar
250g ground almonds
1 tsp baking powder
finely grated zest of 1 large
    orange

FOR THE MASCARPONE FROSTING
250g mascarpone
2 tbsp juice or syrup from the
    can of apricots
finely grated zest of 1 large
    orange

This cake was inspired by exotic holidays in faraway, hot, sunny places... just wishful thinking as it is pouring with rain outside as I make it! My tile decoration is just one idea; you could make it simpler or more complicated. You could even paint on the tile design instead with food colour paste. The cake can be made a day or so ahead, but the tiles should be applied on the day. The tiles can be made weeks ahead, but in that case you may need extra sugarpaste, as I've used and coloured the white sugarpaste that was left over from covering the cake.

TO BAKE
Preheat the oven to 180°C/fan 170°C/350°F/gas mark 4. Lightly butter a 25cm square cake tin and line the base with baking parchment.

To deseed the cardamom pods, split each open with the side of a heavy knife, empty the tiny seeds into a mortar and pestle and grind to a powder. If there are any pieces of husk, sift the powder to remove them. This takes a little time, and can be done a few days beforehand.

Drain the apricots very well, dry with kitchen towel, then mash with a fork. Roast the pistachio nuts on a baking sheet in the oven for about five minutes, cool and roughly chop.

In an electric mixer, whisk the eggs and sugar until pale and foamy; it will take four to six minutes. Start the mixer slowly and increase to medium speed, then beat until the mixture looks like a light mousse. It is important to stop at this point (the whole cake can collapse if the mixture is under- or over-whisked here). Very gently, with a large metal spoon, fold in the almonds, baking powder, orange zest, cardamom powder, apricots and pistachio nuts.

Spoon the batter into the prepared tin and bake for 35–40 minutes, or until a skewer emerges clean. Leave in the tin until completely cold. Carefully remove from the tin and remove the papers; this cake is very fragile as it is flourless. You may find it dips a little in the middle, which is fine. At this stage, you can chill it for a couple of days.

To make the frosting, place the mascarpone in a bowl, beat until smooth, then slowly add the juice or syrup and zest, mixing well.

continued...

TO DECORATE

Place the cake upside down on the drum, sticking it on with a little of the frosting. The cake will probably have dipped a little in the middle, so spread a bit of extra mascarpone frosting to level it. Cover the sides and top with mascarpone frosting.

Knead the sugarpaste to soften, then roll out on a work surface lightly dusted with icing sugar (dust your rolling pin too). Aim for a rough 30cm square about 5mm thick. Wrap very loosely around the rolling pin, place over the cake and gently smooth with your hands. Do not stretch it and work quickly as the paste dries out. Cut away excess all around the base, discarding any that has mascarpone frosting on it, and seal in a polythene bag. You will use this to make the decorations.

Colour half this leftover sugarpaste (about 200g) with ice blue and the rest with egg yellow (see page 168). To make the decorations, roll out the blue sugarpaste to about 2mm thick on a board very lightly dusted with icing sugar. Using the cutter, cut out 42 blue stars and, with a knife, cut out 48 x 5mm blue squares. Next roll out the yellow to 2mm thick and, with the cutter, cut out 12 x 1.5cm squares (I then cut these into a four-sided star by using the tip of the star cutter to make small 'V' shaped cut-outs) and 12 little clover shapes, using the tiny aspic cutter. I also cut out 12 x 6mm yellow squares with a knife, let them dry for an hour or so, painted with edible glue and attached gold leaf. Allow all decorations to dry for at least a couple of hours, as they are then easier to handle.

It is best to work out your tile design before sticking down the pieces, when it is difficult to move them!

Begin with the stars (cutting some in half at the edges) and gradually add the rows of tiny squares and smaller dragees. It is best to do this using a paint brush and edible glue, applying it to each decoration and then positioning it. Finish the cake by sticking one larger gold dragee in the centre of each blue star.

✳ ALSO TRY WITH All-in-one Lemon Cake (see page 61), or Flourless Sachertorte (see page 70), or Madeira Cake (see page 99)

TO DECORATE
1.4kg white sugarpaste
icing sugar, to dust
ice blue food colour paste
egg yellow food colour paste
edible glue
1 sheet edible gold leaf
26 x 2mm gold dragees
39 x 4mm gold dragees

SPECIAL EQUIPMENT
25cm (or larger) square gold cake drum
3cm star cutter
1.5cm square cutter (optional, you can cut squares with a knife if you prefer)
1.4cm clover aspic cutter (from a set)
small paint brush

Pistachio, Grand Marnier and Olive Oil Cake

SERVES 10

125ml green, flavourful extra-virgin olive oil, plus more for the tin
60g raisins (Muscat or Lexia) or sultanas
2 tbsp Grand Marnier, Muscat, Sauternes, or any dessert wine
200g unsalted pistachio nuts, or ground almonds
40g pine nuts
100g plain flour
1 tsp baking powder
200g golden caster sugar
3 eggs, lightly beaten
100g unsalted butter, melted and cooled
finely grated zest of 1 orange
finely grated zest of 2 unwaxed lemons
icing sugar, to dust

Preheat the oven to 170°C/fan 160°C/340°F/gas mark 3½. Lightly oil a 23cm round springform cake tin and line the base with baking parchment. Up to one hour before, if you can, soak the raisins in the Grand Marnier or sweet wine of your choice.

Scatter the pistachio nuts on to one baking tray, and the pine nuts on to another. Roast both trays of nuts for about five minutes, watching the pine nuts carefully as they should only be very lightly coloured. Put the pine nuts to one side. Allow the pistachio nuts to cool, then grind finely in a food processor.

Sift the flour and baking powder into a bowl and add the ground pistachio nuts (or ground almonds).

Place the sugar and eggs into the bowl of an electric mixer (or use a hand-held electric whisk). Whisk on high speed until pale, light and fluffy; this may take up to five minutes. On a slower speed, add the olive oil, butter and zests. Lastly fold in the flour mixture, raisins and any remaining liquid using a large metal spoon.

Turn into the tin, sprinkle over the pine nuts and bake for 35–40 minutes, or until a skewer emerges clean. Rest on a wire rack then turn out of the tin, keeping the top of the cake uppermost. Remove the paper. This cake stores well in an airtight tin for a couple of days. Dust with icing sugar to serve.

This requires a really good-quality olive oil, Grand Marnier or a dessert wine of your choice. You will only use a couple of tablespoons in the recipe, but the wine will be a perfect accompaniment to the cake, should you choose to use it. Pistachio nuts or almonds – the choice is yours – result in very different cakes. Ground almonds make a lighter cake, whereas pistachio nuts give a denser, beautifully pale green crumb.

Box of Chocolates
FLOURLESS SACHERTORTE

SERVES 25 BIG OR 36 SMALL
PORTIONS

FOR THE CAKE
260g unsalted butter, diced, plus
more for the tin
300g 70% cocoa solids chocolate,
chopped
8 eggs, separated
250g golden caster sugar
2 tsp vanilla extract
pinch of salt
340g ground almonds
6 tbsp apricot jam, to glaze

FOR THE CHOCOLATE GANACHE
300g 70% cocoa solids chocolate,
broken into pieces
270ml double cream
60g unsalted butter

TO DECORATE
a box of your favourite
chocolates

SPECIAL EQUIPMENT
25cm square thin cake board
a beautiful ribbon (optional)

A sensational dark and very grown-up
cake. It is not a classic version of the
famous Viennese Sachertorte, but all
the more moist and rich. Decorate
with your favourite chocolates, and
don't count calories! This cake is so
moist that it keeps well for days and
freezes brilliantly.

Preheat the oven to 160°C/fan 150°C/325°F/gas mark 3. Lightly butter
a 25cm square tin and line the base with baking parchment.

Melt the chocolate and butter in a heatproof bowl over very gently
simmering water, making sure the bowl does not touch the water. Set
aside to cool.

Put the egg yolks into the bowl of an electric mixer or a large mixing
bowl, and the egg whites into a clean, grease-free bowl. Add the sugar
and vanilla to the egg yolks and whisk until the mixture is thickened
and creamy (the 'ribbon' stage). This may take three or four minutes.

Turn the mixer to low (or a hand-held whisk on a lower speed) and
add the cooled, melted chocolate and butter. Separately whisk the
egg whites with the salt to stiff peaks. With a metal spoon, fold the
almonds into the chocolate mixture, then add a large spoonful of egg
whites. Once combined, fold in the rest of the egg whites, very, very
gently, a large spoonful at a time.

Turn the cake mixture into the prepared tin and bake for 45–50
minutes, or until a skewer emerges clean. Take from the oven, leave
for a couple of minutes in the tin, then turn out on to a wire rack and
remove the papers.

Warm the apricot jam in a small pan and press it through a sieve.
Brush all over the cake while both jam and cake are still warm.

Turn the cake on to the thin cake board, and put it on a wire rack.
Place a sheet of baking parchment underneath to catch the drips.

To make the ganache, melt the chocolate, cream and butter in a
heatproof bowl set over very gently simmering water, making sure the
bowl does not touch the water. Stir until smooth, then allow it to cool
a little to thicken before pouring over the cake. Allow
to set for at least two hours before decorating with the
chocolates and ribbon, if using.

✱ ALSO TRY WITH Banoffee Cake (see page 42), or
All-in-one Chocolate Cake, for a less intense chocolate
cake suitable for a child (see page 77), or Madeira Cake
(see page 99)

Erupting Volcano

MARBLE CAKE

SERVES 20

FOR THE CAKE
1 x Marble Cake recipe
(see page 187)
1 x Chocolate Buttercream recipe
(see page 187)

FOR THE HONEYCOMB LAVA
200g golden syrup
350g caster sugar
2 tbsp distilled white vinegar
2 tsp bicarbonate of soda

TO DECORATE AND ASSEMBLE
200g granulated sugar
mint green food colour paste
3 tbsp royal icing
30cm round cake drum
200g milk chocolate, chopped
red or orange boiled sweets
4 packets popping candy
400g digestive biscuits, crushed
plastic dinosaurs
1 firework candle (or indoor
sparkler fireworks)

Light the firework candle at the centre of this spectacular cake and await the applause.

For the lava, line a 23cm baking tray with baking parchment. Have a glass of cold water to hand. In a large, heavy-based pan, place the syrup, sugar, vinegar and 125ml water. On a gentle heat, stir until the sugar dissolves. Increase the heat, bring to a boil and do not stir any more. If you have a sugar thermometer, boil it to 155°C. If not, drop a small ball of syrup into the glass of water. If it crackles and becomes a hard ball, it is ready. If not, boil until it is. Remove from the heat and add the bicarbonate of soda; it will erupt! Let it calm down, stir and pour into the prepared tray. Leave to set, then break into chunks. You won't need it all for the cake. It keeps for a few days in a dry, airtight tin. Crush 100g of it in a polythene bag with a rolling pin.

For the grass, place the granulated sugar into a bowl. Mix a little green food colour with 2 tsp water in a bowl and pour into the sugar. Mix with your fingers and spread on a tray to dry. Mix every couple of hours. In a dry place, this keeps for weeks.

Give the cakes a spell in the fridge to make them easier to shape. Trim all three so the tops are level. Cut each in half horizontally to give six cakes. Sandwich together with the buttercream. Stick a skewer into the top right through to the work surface, to use as a guide to avoid a lopsided volcano. Shape the cake from the top. Volcanoes do vary in shape; mine has a flat plateau on top and gently sloping edges. When you are happy, dig out a crater in which to place the candle.

To assemble the cake, spread a thin layer of royal icing over the drum and press on the sugar 'grass'. Remember, you won't see the middle, so concentrate on the edges. Place the cake on to the drum.

Melt the milk chocolate in a small bowl over simmering water, making sure the bowl does not touch the water. Cool slightly. Pour over the cake. Press on the crushed honeycomb and a few crushed boiled sweets for the embers, with the popping candy. Let the honeycomb tumble over the board. Surround the tableau with biscuit crumbs. Position the dinosaurs around and the firework candle in the crater.

✶ ALSO TRY WITH All-in-one Chocolate Cake (see page 77), or Toffee Cake (see page 187)

Sugar Fossils

MAKES 10
Colour 200g white sugarpaste grey with black food colour paste (see page 168). On a work top dusted with icing sugar, roll out the sugarpaste to 5mm thick. Using a 5.5cm round cutter, cut out discs. Press a toy plastic beetle or fly into each one. Leave to dry.

Chocolate Dinosaurs
CHOCOLATE SHORTBREAD

I made countless visits to the Natural History Museum with my son to view the dinosaur skeletons, his earliest fascination. These are in memory of those times, Hari.

Line two or three baking trays with baking parchment. Preheat the oven to 170°C/fan 160°C/340°F/gas mark 3½. Lightly dust a board and rolling pin with flour and roll out the dough to about 4mm thick. Cut out a selection of dinosaurs, re-roll the excess and cut out more until all the dough is used. Lay on to the baking trays, chill for 30 minutes, then bake for 12–15 minutes. Leave on the trays until cool.

To decorate, colour half the sugarpaste green (see page 168), with mostly mint green and a little Christmas green. Colour the remainder blue with mainly ice blue and a little navy. Dust a board with icing sugar and roll out the green sugarpaste to 2mm thick. Cut out using the dinosaur cutters, cutting exactly the same shapes as the biscuits. Sprinkle a little icing sugar over the biscuits and flick over a tiny amount of water (you do not want soggy biscuits) to create a 'glue'. (Or use royal icing, or brush with edible glue.) Stick the sugarpaste dinosaurs on the biscuits. To decorate, pipe on dots and lines with royal icing. If you want, brush a small area on each biscuit with edible glue and sprinkle over the glitter. With a dry brush, remove excess.

✱ ALSO TRY WITH Vanilla Shortbread (see page 186)

MAKES 36

TO BAKE
plain flour, to dust
1 x Chocolate Shortbread dough (see page 27)

TO DECORATE
500g white sugarpaste
mint green food colour paste
Christmas green food colour paste
ice blue food colour paste
navy food colour paste
icing sugar, to dust
60g bag white royal icing, no. 1 nozzle
edible glue (optional)
edible clear glitter (optional)

SPECIAL EQUIPMENT
1 set dinosaur cutters (mine are 12–15cm)
paint brush (optional)

Peanut Choc Caramel Cookies

Preheat the oven to 170°C/fan 160°C/340°F/gas mark 3½. Line two baking trays with baking parchment. Beat the butter and sugar until fluffy. Add the syrup and beat. Add the flour, chocolate drops, peanuts and toffee and mix gently with your hands, or a large spoon.

Lightly flour your hands and divide into 20 balls. Space out well on the trays. Squash the centre down with your fingers and bake for 10–12 minutes, or until cooked at the sides but gooey in the middle. After a few minutes, remove to a wire rack. These will keep a few days in an airtight tin (if well hidden!).

MAKES 20

100g unsalted butter, softened
100g light muscovado sugar
1 tbsp golden syrup
150g self-raising flour, sifted, plus more to dust
100g milk chocolate drops (or dark if you prefer)
80g roasted, salted peanuts, quite finely chopped
50g soft toffee, fudge or butterscotch, finely chopped

Football Boots
ALL-IN-ONE CHOCOLATE CAKE

Guaranteed to delight a football fan when made in their team's colours. If you have real football boots to copy, it will make these more realistic. Think of the All-in-one Chocolate Cake here a bit as you would a little black dress: bring it out for any occasion, and dress it up or down as mood dictates. Serve it at a children's party, or fill with one of the icings below for a sophisticated celebration.

TO BAKE

Preheat the oven to 180°C/fan 170°C/350°F/gas mark 4. Butter a 20cm, 7.5cm deep square tin and line the base with baking parchment. Sift the flour and baking powder into a bowl, add the butter, eggs, sugar, vanilla and cocoa paste. Beat together but do not over-mix. Scrape into the tin. Bake for 35–40 minutes, or until a skewer emerges clean. Remove from the oven, leave for a few minutes, then turn on to a wire rack to cool completely. Remove the papers.

For the buttercream, melt the chocolate, if using, in a small heatproof bowl over simmering water, making sure the bowl does not touch the water. Cool. Beat the butter until pale and fluffy and add the icing sugar, vanilla and cocoa, if using. Beat for five minutes. Add the chocolate, if using, and beat again. It will thicken if you keep beating.

ALTERNATIVE ICINGS TO TRY

CARAMEL FROSTING
200ml carton double cream, lightly whipped
4 tbsp dulce de leche (or caramel spread)
Fold the cream and caramel together lightly so that it is marbled.

CHOCOLATE GANACHE
150g 70% cocoa solids chocolate
150g sour cream
Melt the chocolate over simmering water and mix into the cream.

MOCHA
250g mascarpone
2 tbsp dark muscovado sugar
1 tsp strong coffee, cooled
Beat the mascarpone, then beat in the sugar and coffee.

SERVES 8

FOR THE CAKE
225g unsalted butter, really soft, diced, plus more for the tins
180g self-raising flour
1 tsp baking powder
4 eggs, lightly beaten
225g golden caster sugar
1 tsp vanilla extract
3 tbsp cocoa powder, mixed to a loose paste with 3–4 tbsp boiling water and cooled

FOR THE BUTTERCREAM
100g 70% cocoa solids chocolate, chopped, or 2 tbsp cocoa powder
150g unsalted butter, really soft
200g icing sugar, sifted
1 tsp vanilla extract

continued...

840g white sugarpaste

Christmas red food colour paste

baby blue food colour paste

liquorice food colour paste

(or 600g ready-made blue
    sugarpaste, 200g ready-made
    black sugarpaste, and 40g
    ready-made red sugarpaste)

icing sugar, to dust

30g bag white royal icing

2 liquorice strips, each about
    75cm long (I used two
    liquorice pinwheels, unwound)

chocolate footballs

SPECIAL EQUIPMENT

20cm square thin card

3cm star cutter

TO DECORATE

If you are colouring your own sugarpaste, remove 40g and colour it red (see page 168). Next, colour 600g blue and the final 200g black. Give the cake a spell in the fridge, to make it easier to shape.

Make a football boot template, about 20cm long. Cut the card into two football boots, using the template; don't forget to turn it over so you have one left and one right foot! Place the template on top of the cake and cut it into shape, straight down towards the board. Cut an oval about 10x4cm in the back of each shoe (where the ankle goes) and scoop out the cake. Slope the front half of the shoe down towards the toe and the edges (it helps to have a real boot to copy). Stick each boot to its card with a little buttercream, then cover with buttercream.

Next, on a work surface dusted with icing sugar, roll out half the blue sugarpaste to a 5mm thick rectangle about 28x18cm. Lift on to one of the boots and gently ease over, pressing into the foot hole and moulding around the sides. Repeat with the other boot and rub and smooth all over until you are happy with the shapes. To make the insides of the boots, roll out two black ovals of sugarpaste about 10x6cm. Pipe royal icing into the two cavities and press into place. Cut two small ovals of black sugarpaste for the tongues (about 6x2cm) and again stick in place on the front of the boots. Roll two large 'U' shapes for the laces panel in blue sugarpaste, each 1.5cm thick and 9cm long, wider towards the foot hole end, and position using royal icing.

Using a cocktail stick, make stitch markings all around the inside and outside. Make five holes with a skewer either side for the laces. Cut the liquorice laces into eight 4cm strips and press into the holes. Cut the remaining liquorice to form the four long laces. Cut a triangle from blue sugarpaste about 6x5x5cm and cut off the point to form the flap. Stick into place, making stitch holes again with a cocktail stick. Roll out the red sugarpaste and cut out two stars and two 14x1.5cm strips to make the flashes at the back of each boot. Stick on with royal icing.

For the studs, roll out some black sugarpaste into a thin sausage and cut into 22 balls. Mould into studs and place under each of the boards, sticking around the heel, the front, and the edges, where they will be visible. Fill each boot with chocolate footballs.

✶ ALSO TRY WITH Victoria Sponge (see page 109)

Little Monsters
ALL-IN-ONE ORANGE CAKE

MAKES 16

16 cupcake cases
1 x All-in-one Lemon Cake
    batter (all lemon changed to
    oranges, but juice of ½ large
    orange only in cake, see
    page 61)

FOR THE SYRUP (OPTIONAL)
juice of 1 orange
5 tbsp caster sugar

FOR THE ICING
500g icing sugar, sifted
5–6 tbsp orange or lemon juice

TO MAKE THE MONSTERS
500g white sugarpaste (or ready
    mixed colours of your choice)
The colours I used were:
    pink food colour paste
    green food colour paste
    red food colour paste
    yellow food colour paste
    blue food colour paste
    violet food colour paste
    orange food colour paste
    black food colour paste
60g piping bag white royal icing,
    no. 1 nozzle

The more revolting and gruesome the better! Thank you
to Molly and Jacob Eardley (aged 11 and 8) for designing
the originals for me to copy. I have listed the colours and
quantities of icing I used, but this is only a rough guide.
A great way to get children involved: just give them the
icing, colours, a piping bag or two (and this photo to
spark their imaginations) and leave them for an hour or
two! You could use food colouring pens too (although the
sugarpaste will need to have dried overnight first).

TO BAKE
To bake the cupcakes, line two cupcake tins with the paper cases.
Divide the batter between the cases. Bake for 15–18 minutes, or until
the cakes spring back to the touch. Meanwhile, if you are making
the syrup, mix the orange juice and sugar in a bowl. Immediately the
cakes come from the oven, prick holes all over each with a cocktail
stick and douse with syrup. (Only do this after they are defrosted, if
the cakes have been frozen.) Leave to cool completely in the tins.

When ready to ice, place the icing sugar in a bowl and gradually add
just enough orange juice to make a pourable consistency which coats
the back of a spoon. Pour a spoonful or so of the icing over each cake,
gently easing it over the cake with a spoon so it spreads to the edges.
Allow to set for an hour or so.

TO DECORATE
Divide the white sugarpaste into however many colours you wish to
use (each of my monsters took 20–30g) and colour it (see page 168),
keeping back a little white for the eyes and teeth. Make your monsters!
Stick the monster parts together with royal icing, and decorate each
cake with a monster, adhering with a blob of royal icing, if necessary.

★ ALSO TRY WITH All-in-one Chocolate Cake (see page 77), or
Liquorice Toffee Cupcakes (see page 160)

Mojito or Pina Colada Cheesecakes

MAKES 6 MARTINI GLASSES, OR 12
'CUPCAKE' CHEESECAKES

FOR THE BASE
180g plain digestive biscuits
60g unsalted butter, melted
2–3 tbsp finely chopped mint
12 strong foil cupcakes cases
    (optional)

FOR THE MOJITO
grated zest and juice of 4 limes
8 tbsp chopped mint

FOR THE CHEESECAKE
300g double cream
4 tbsp rum
400g cream cheese
300g mascarpone
120g golden caster sugar

FOR THE PINA COLADA
100g pineapple, finely diced
80g desiccated coconut

TO DECORATE
sprigs of mint
glacé cherries
pineapple wedges
paper umbrellas
indoor sparklers

MOJITO CHEESECAKES

To make the bases, crush the digestive biscuits in a food processor, or in a sealed polythene bag with a rolling pin. Tip the crumbs into a bowl and add the butter and mint. Divide between the cocktail glasses or foil cases and press down firmly with the back of a teaspoon. Chill in the fridge for at least half an hour.

Place the lime zest and juice and the mint in a small saucepan over a low heat until just warm to a finger, then set aside for a couple of hours to infuse. Strain. Very lightly whip the double cream until only just thickened, adding the rum slowly towards the end.

In a bowl, beat together the cream cheese, mascarpone and sugar, then beat together with the cream. With a large metal spoon, fold in the lime juice mixture; try not to over-mix. Divide between the glasses or foil cases and chill to set for at least a couple of hours. Arrange on a large tray (mirrored would look fabulous) or pile high on a cake stand. Decorate as you wish just before serving.

PINA COLADA CHEESECAKES

Make the base in the same way as for the Mojito cheesecakes, omitting the mint.

Make the cheesecake mixture as above, omitting the lime juice mixture. Fold in the pineapple and coconut.

Divide between the glasses or foil cases and chill to set for at least a couple of hours. Decorate as you wish just before serving.

Sure to be the talking point of any fashionable party, serve these alongside the cocktails! No baking required and dead simple to make. I know piña colada is as deeply unfashionable as mojito is on trend, but you just might change your mind by making them: pineapple, coconut and rum is a great flavour combination. Make these either in your favourite cocktail glasses or in strong, foil cupcake cases.

Pirate Galleon
ALL-IN-ONE CHOCOLATE CAKE

SERVES 20-24

2 x 20cm square, 7.5cm deep
    All-in-one Chocolate Cakes
    (see page 77)
1½ x Chocolate Buttercream
    recipe (see page 77)

SPECIAL EQUIPMENT
40cm round or square cake drum
8 wooden skewers (or plastic
    dowelling rods)
wood grain-textured mat
    (optional)

TO DECORATE
icing sugar, to dust
250g light brown sugarpaste
    (or white sugarpaste and
    brown food colour paste)
10 mint rings
10 chocolate caramels
2–3 tea bags
3 sheets 13x8cm white paper
pirate food picks
    (see suppliers, p188)
glue
pirate candles
    (see suppliers, p188)

Pirates and Treasure Island are such popular themes for small boys' parties that this is certain to be a huge success. It's not difficult to make. Do make sure you use skewers to support the boat... my first attempt capsized!

Give the cakes a spell in the fridge or freezer, to make them easier to mould. Trim the surfaces of the cakes if necessary, to ensure they are flat. Cut both squares in half lengthways so that you have four cakes, each 20cm long and 10cm wide. Take two halves and buttercream together, making sure the top surface is the flat base of a cake. This is the central part of the galleon. Place on the drum.

Take a third cake and cut it into three pieces, each measuring 10x6cm. Using plenty of buttercream, stick these at the back of the boat with the top of one slightly set back. Secure with three skewers or dowels and cut them to the same level of the cake so you don't see them.

For the front of the boat, cut three triangles from the final cake. Mine measured 10x9x9cm. Using plenty of buttercream, sandwich together, stick to the front and secure with two more skewers. Carve away the front and sides lightly to make a boat shape.

Spread buttercream all over the cake. On a clean work surface dusted with icing sugar, roll out the light brown sugarpaste to about 3mm thick. You will need to cut several 4cm-wide strips to go all around the boat, pressed in the wood grain mat first, if using. The two middle lengths of the ship are 20cm, 30cm to wrap around the front and another 30cm for the back. Make a coil of sugarpaste for the helm and press on, using buttercream to adhere if necessary. Press five mints into the buttercream each side for the portholes and, using buttercream, attach the chocolate caramel 'cannons' to the sugarpaste.

Wet a tea bag, squeeze out most of the water, and wipe it all over all the sheets of paper. Allow to dry, then cut out six sails. The front four sails measure 13x8cm and the two at the back are slightly smaller. Attach two sails to each of the three remaining skewers, then press them into the cake. Remove the small sticks from pirate food picks and glue to the tops of the skewers. Position the pirate candles. Finally, write a birthday message on one of the sails. Your ship is ready to sail!

★ ALSO TRY WITH Madeira Cake (see page 99)

Giant Jam Sandwich Biscuits

MAKES THREE 15CM BISCUITS

FOR THE BISCUITS

250g plain flour, plus plenty
    to dust
50g cornflour
100g icing sugar, plus more to
    dust (optional)
250g unsalted butter, softened
    and diced
1 egg yolk
1 tsp vanilla extract
6 tbsp strawberry jam, or lemon
    curd, or caramel spread

SPECIAL EQUIPMENT
5cm heart cutter
paint brush

You can freeze this dough, or make the biscuits a day
ahead. Only dust with icing sugar just before serving.

Preheat the oven to 170°C/fan 160°C/340°F/gas mark 3½.

In a large bowl, sift the flour, cornflour and icing sugar together. Rub
in the butter with your fingertips until the mixture resembles crumbs.
Add the egg yolk and vanilla extract. Gently bring into a ball, wrap in
cling film and rest in the fridge for 30 minutes or so, as this buttery
biscuit dough is very soft and needs to firm up.

On a very well-floured board, with a floured rolling pin, roll out half
the dough to 4mm thick. If the dough is too soft to work with easily,
place the board of rolled-out dough into the fridge (room permitting!)
to firm up for 30 minutes or so. Cut out three circles at a time using
a 15cm baking tin or a plate as a guide. Repeat with the remaining
dough. Cut a heart shape from the centre of three of the biscuits.

Place the biscuits on two or three baking sheets lined with baking
parchment and, using the end of a paint brush, make a pattern all
around the edges. Rest in the fridge or at room temperature for about
30 minutes. Bake for 12–15 minutes, re-cut the central hearts straight
away if necessary, and cool on the baking tray; don't try to move them
until they're cold!

If the jam is not smooth, warm it slightly in a small pan, then press
through a sieve to remove any lumps. Let it cool completely. Spread
2 tbsp jam on to each of the whole biscuits, and dust those with heart-
shaped holes with icing sugar, if you like. Place the tops of the biscuits
on the bases.

✷ ALSO TRY WITH Vanilla Shortbread (see page 186)

Fresh Flower Heart
HONEY CAKE

TO COLOUR THE SUGARPASTE AND BAKE
First of all, colour the sugarpaste to your chosen colour (see page 168). I mixed both ice blue and mint green to create an eau de nil colour.

Preheat the oven to 170°C/fan 160°C/340°F/gas mark 3½. Lightly butter the heart-shaped tin and line the base and sides with a double layer of baking parchment. This cake has a high sugar content with both sugar and honey, and the sides can catch easily; the baking parchment will protect it.

Pour the cake batter into the prepared tin and bake for 55-60 minutes, or until a skewer emerges clean. Remove from the oven and leave in the tin for a couple of minutes. Run a knife around the edges and tip out on to a wire rack to cool. Remove the papers.

When the cake is cold, trim the top surface level, turn it upside down, and attach it to the board with a little buttercream. Spread the remaining buttercream all over the top and sides of the cake.

TO DECORATE
On a large clean work surface dusted with icing sugar, roll out the sugarpaste to 5mm thick and large enough to cover the top and sides of the cake. Keep moving the sugarpaste and run a palette knife underneath it from time to time, adding more icing sugar if necessary. Roll loosely around the rolling pin and lift it on to the cake. Smooth it all over, rubbing with your hands, and cut away the excess. Any sugarpaste that is clean, and does not have crumbs or buttercream on can be kept, sealed in a polythene bag, for another time.

Wrap the ribbon around the cake and attach at the back seam: either tie together neatly, use a blob of buttercream or a small piece of sticky tape.

When ready to display, decorate with the fresh flowers of your choice. Please do ensure that they are scrupulously clean and dry, as droplets of water will spoil the smooth finish of your icing.

✶ ALSO TRY WITH Flourless Sachertorte (see page 70), or Madeira Cake (see page 99), or Tiramisu Cake (see page 155), or Masala Chai Cake (see page 184)

SERVES 16–20

FOR THE CAKE AND DECORATION
1.5kg white sugarpaste
ice blue food colour paste
mint green food colour paste
unsalted butter, for the tin
1 x Honey Cake batter
   (see page 183)
1 x Honey Buttercream recipe
   (see page 183)
icing sugar, to dust
fresh edible flowers of your
   choice

SPECIAL EQUIPMENT
25cm (at widest point) heart-
   shaped cake tin
30cm heart-shaped board
   (or round or square)
1 metre ribbon of your choice

A scattering of unsprayed edible flowers or petals is the quickest way to produce a stunning cake with minimum fuss. I have used violets here. You could also try rose petals, roses, primulas and pansies, cornflowers, lavender, marigolds, small sunflowers, carnations or nasturtiums.

Beside the Seaside – A Bucket Cake

NEAPOLITAN SPONGE CAKE

SERVES 24

FOR THE CAKE
450g unsalted butter, softened, diced, plus more for the tins
450g self-raising flour
2 tsp baking powder
8 eggs, lightly beaten
2 tsp vanilla extract
450g golden caster sugar
pink food colour paste
1 tbsp cocoa powder

FOR THE BUTTERCREAM
350g unsalted butter
2 tsp vanilla extract
350g icing sugar, sifted

A fun, life-size bucket, perfect for a summer party. Made with a Neopolitan sponge for a full-on seaside experience.

TO BAKE

Preheat the oven to 180°C/fan 170°C/350°F/gas mark 4. Butter three 20cm round tins and line the bases with baking parchment. If you only have two 20cm round tins, then make the full amount of cake batter, divide by three and leave one-third in a bowl. Bake it as soon as a tin becomes free. I use an electric mixer and beater attachment, but use a food processor, or a bowl and electric whisk, if you prefer.

First, sift the flour and baking powder into a bowl, and add the butter, eggs, vanilla and sugar. Beat until well blended, but do not over-mix, as you want a light sponge. Divide between three bowls. Leave one bowl of mixture as it is (for the vanilla layer) and mix a few drops of pink food colour into the second. For the third, mix the cocoa powder with 1–2 tbsp hot water to make a paste, allow to cool, then add to the batter. Put each colour into a separate prepared tin.

Bake each cake for 30–35 minutes, or until a skewer emerges clean. Remove from the oven and leave for a couple of minutes. Run a knife around the rim to loosen the cake from the tin, remove the papers and leave to cool completely.

For the buttercream, beat the butter in an electric mixer until really pale and fluffy, then add the vanilla and icing sugar and beat for at least five minutes more until really creamy.

TO ASSEMBLE

Cut each of the three cakes in half horizontally. Take a chocolate layer and place it, cut side up, on a work surface. Take a vanilla layer, spread a layer of buttercream on the uncut side and place on top. (It is much easier to spread the buttercream on the uncut side as you will have fewer crumbs.) Repeat with a pink layer. Now repeat the process, ensuring that the layer at the very top of the cake is uncut side up.

Now give the cake a spell in the fridge or freezer; even an hour will help enormously. You will find it far easier to shape, especially when very fresh. With a very sharp or serrated knife, cut the cake into a bucket shape. Leave the top as it is but shape the middle and bottom tiers, so the cake tapers to be slightly narrower at the bottom. Slightly hollow out the very top as it will need a layer of sand!

Cover the cake with most of the remaining buttercream, keeping back a couple of tablespoons. Place it on to your cake drum or platter.

TO DECORATE

Colour the sugarpaste your chosen colour (see page 168), keeping back a small piece (about 100g) for the white handle and the two flower hinges. Seal the white and blue sugarpastes separately in polythene bags. Dust a work surface with icing sugar, then roll out less than half the blue sugarpaste into a 35x12cm rectangle about 5mm thick. Wrap around the front half of the bucket. Repeat for the back of the bucket, manipulating the sugarpaste with your hands and rubbing it to smooth out imperfections. Cut away any excess.

For the top of the bucket, roll out a circle slightly larger than the top of the cake (use the cake tin as a template), about 5mm thick, and lift on to the cake. Press down gently into the slightly dipped centre. Seal the rim of the bucket as neatly as you can, pinching together with your fingers and rubbing away any imperfections.

To make the handle, roll out a long, thin strip (35x1cm) of white sugarpaste and attach to the sides with a little royal icing.

Cut two flower hinges with a piece of the remaining white sugarpaste. Add a little yellow food colour to a tiny piece of sugarpaste and make two balls, each about 1cm wide, for the centre of the flower hinges. Stick them on to each of the flower hinges with royal icing. Stick the hinges on the cake where the handle meets the bucket, on both sides, again using a little royal icing to adhere.

In a large polythene bag, crush the biscuits by bashing them with a rolling pin (small hands will be very willing!). Spread the reserved buttercream into the top of the bucket, sprinkle with biscuit 'sand' and scatter the rest all around the bucket. Arrange the pebbles, shrimps and shells all around. You can now choose to stick the spade in the top of the cake, or even use it as a serving utensil.

✱ ALSO TRY WITH All-in-one Lemon Cake (see page 61), or Madeira Cake (see page 99), or Victoria Sponge (see page 109), or Liquorice Toffee Cake (see page 160)

TO DECORATE

1.4kg white sugarpaste
ice blue food colour paste (or any colour, for the bucket)
icing sugar, to dust
60g bag white royal icing
yellow food colour paste
250g plain digestive biscuits
sugar pebbles and shrimps
chocolate shells
1 toy spade, scrupulously cleaned

SPECIAL EQUIPMENT
35cm round cake drum or platter
3cm blossom cutter

Over the Rainbow

HIDDEN FRUIT AND VEG CAKES

MAKES 80–90 TINY FAIRY
(MINI MUFFIN) CAKES,
OR 36 FAIRY CAKES

FOR THE CAKES
80–90 mini muffin paper cases,
    or 36 fairy cake cases
350g self-raising flour
1 tsp baking powder
2 tsp ground cinnamon
½ tsp salt
1 tsp ground ginger
80ml whole milk
120ml sunflower oil
230g light muscovado sugar
3 large eggs, lightly beaten
300g prepared fruit or vegetables.
    Choose from: blueberries;
    courgette (roughly grated and
    excess moisture removed);
    apple (skinned, cored and
    grated); parsnip (peeled and
    grated); carrot (peeled and
    grated); or banana (roughly
    chopped)

FOR THE FROSTING
240g icing sugar, sifted
500g cream cheese
juice of up to 1½ lemons
natural liquid food colours: blue,
    green, yellow, pink, red

I always struggled to get my children to eat fruit and veg when they were small. But these bite-sized cakes are packed full of goodness and iced with a delicious cream cheese frosting in a rainbow of colours. I used natural food colours which are now available in some supermarkets, containing beetroot, paprika, turmeric, tomatoes and grape skins (even algae). One word of caution: don't make the colours too strong as you may then be able to detect some of those flavours! If you would like more than one flavour of cake, make up one cake mix, divide it into two or three, and add 150g each of two different fruit or vegetables, or 100g each of three.

Preheat the oven to 170°C/fan 160°C/340°F/gas mark 3½. Line as many small-hole baking trays as you have with paper cases. (Or line three fairy cake trays with fairy cake cases.) Sift together the flour, baking powder, cinnamon, salt and ginger. In a large bowl, beat together the milk, oil, sugar and eggs. Prepare your chosen vegetables or fruit. Make sure they are very well dried to avoid soggy cakes!

Beat the flour mixture into the wet ingredients, taking care not to over-mix, then fold in the vegetables or fruit. Spoon into the cases and bake for eight to 10 minutes, or until they spring back to the touch. You may need to bake them in batches. Cool on a wire rack. (If you are making fairy cakes, they need to be baked for 15–20 minutes.)

To make the frosting, beat the icing sugar into the cream cheese. Gradually add the lemon juice, to taste, then divide into six little bowls. Colour each bowl a different colour of the rainbow, mixing the food colours to achieve the orange and purple tones.

Divide the little cakes into six equal groups. Spread the frosting on to the cakes with a small blunt knife. You will have at least 12 of each colour. These cakes need to be iced on the day they are to be eaten, though the un-iced cakes freeze well, if you need to get ahead.

✱ ALSO TRY WITH All-in-one Lemon Cake (see page 61), or All-in-one Chocolate Cake (see page 77)

Alice in Wonderland's Unbirthday Party

Alice's Teapot
MADEIRA CAKE

TO COLOUR THE SUGARPASTE AND BAKE

Cut away 100g of the white sugarpaste and set aside, sealed in a polythene bag, to make the little flower decorations. Colour the remaining sugarpaste pale blue, using baby blue and a very small amount of navy food colour (see page 168). Seal the coloured sugarpaste in a polythene bag. Colour the Mexican modelling paste the same pale blue for the handle and spout of the teapot. (Or, if you prefer, you can make these from coloured card.) Dust a work surface with icing sugar, then roll out the modelling paste to about 4mm thick; cut out the spout and handle using the templates. Dry overnight, or even better, two days ahead, to harden completely.

Preheat the oven to 160°C/fan 150°C/325°F/gas mark 3.

Butter the cake tin very well indeed. Place a piece of baking parchment over the hole in the base of one of the semi-spherical halves. Make a stand of twisted aluminium foil to stop the tin from rolling around in the oven, and stand the other on the base supplied.

Sift the flour, cornflour and salt together. Using the beater attachment of an electric mixer, or a bowl and electric whisk, beat together the eggs, sugar and lemon zest until light and fluffy and slightly thickened (this may take a good five minutes). Very gently fold in the crème fraîche, then the flour mixture, the butter and lastly the lemon juice.

Divide the batter between the prepared tins, level the surfaces and bake for 35–40 minutes, or until a skewer emerges clean. Meanwhile, make the lemon syrup by mixing the sugar and lemon juice in a bowl.

As soon as the cakes come from the oven, place on wire racks and, after a few minutes, run a knife between the cakes and tins and turn them out. If you buttered the tins well, then they should be perfect! Brush the syrup over the warm cakes and allow to cool completely.

To make the lemon buttercream, in an electric mixer, or with a hand-held electric whisk, beat the butter until really pale and fluffy. Add the icing sugar and lemon zest and continue to beat for about another five minutes until light and fluffy. Add the lemon juice gradually and keep beating, tasting as you add it. You may not need it all.

SERVES 20 (OR MAYBE IT
   DOESN'T…)

FOR THE SUGARPASTE
1kg white sugarpaste
baby blue food colour paste
navy food colour paste
100g Mexican modelling paste
   (see suppliers, page 188)
icing sugar, to dust

SPECIAL EQUIPMENT
handle and spout cardboard
   templates (see page 100)
2-litre spherical cake tin
   (see suppliers, page 188)

FOR THE MADEIRA CAKE
100g unsalted butter, melted and
   cooled, plus more for the tin
250g self-raising flour, sifted
30g cornflour
pinch of salt
4 free-range eggs, lightly beaten
300g golden caster sugar
finely grated zest and juice
   of 1 unwaxed lemon
150ml crème fraîche

FOR THE LEMON SYRUP
100g golden caster sugar
juice of 1 large lemon

FOR THE LEMON BUTTERCREAM
250g unsalted butter, softened
250g icing sugar, sifted
finely grated zest and juice
   of 2 unwaxed lemons

continued...

TO ASSEMBLE

15cm thin card cake board, cut
   down to a 12cm round
30cm round cake drum
   (optional)
icing sugar, to dust
60g bag white royal icing,
   no. 1 nozzle
4 flower cutters (mine were
   2.5cm and 1.5cm blossoms,
   and 2cm and 1.5cm daisies)

TO ASSEMBLE

Trim the two tops of both cakes if necessary, so they are flat. Cut each in half horizontally, to give four layers. Cut a small amount from the base, to stop it rolling around. Sandwich the layers together with half the lemon buttercream. Adhere the base to the cake board with a little buttercream. Spread the remaining buttercream over the entire ball. Place the cake on the cake drum, if using.

Knead the blue sugarpaste on a work surface dusted with icing sugar. Once malleable, roll it into a large circle 35–40cm in diameter and 5–6mm thick. Roll loosely around the rolling pin, and place over the cake. Ease it around the cake, rubbing with your hands and smoothing away imperfections. Press in around the base and cut away excess. While it is still soft, indent a line to insert the spout and two opposite for the handle. As this is an Alice teapot, I made it at a slight angle with the spout slightly in the air.

Make the lid by rolling out a 9.5cm circle of blue sugarpaste. Place a small ball of sugarpaste underneath to raise the lid up, and stick it on top of the teapot with royal icing. To make the flowers, roll out the white sugarpaste on a work surface dusted with icing sugar to about 2mm thick. Cut out about 40 small and 18 larger flowers. Make the single small white rose for the top (see page 121), using about 20g of the white sugarpaste.

Using royal icing, stick on all the little flowers, the rose and, if you wish, pipe on stems, leaves and spots. Pipe white dots into the centres of the flowers. Push the spout and handle into the slots in the teapot, using royal icing to hold them in place.

✱ ALSO TRY WITH Banoffee Cake (see page 42), or All-in-one Chocolate Cake (see page 77), or Victoria Sponge (see page 109)

HANDLE

SPOUT

Alice's Cups and Saucers
VANILLA SHORTBREAD

Amazingly simple, especially if you use bought biscuits and sugar flowers.

The day before, divide the sugarpaste into three and colour one-third pale pink, the second pale blue and the last pale yellow (see page 168). Make 48 handles, by rolling out thin 7cm sausages of sugarpaste and curling into an 'S' shape. Leave the handles to dry overnight.

Next day, preheat the oven to 170°C/fan 160°C/340°F/gas mark 3½. Roll out the shortbread to 4mm thick on a floured surface and cut into 5cm circles. Place on baking trays lined with baking parchment and bake for eight to 10 minutes. Leave on the trays to cool.

Lay the biscuits out on a board. On a clean board dusted with icing sugar, roll one of the colours of sugarpaste to about 2mm thick and cut out a few circles and blossoms. Repeat with the other colours until you have 48 circles and 48 blossoms. Using royal icing, stick the circles to the biscuits, then stick a marshmallow and a Jazzie on top. Attach a handle and blossom to each cup, piping a centre into each blossom.

MAKES 48 CUPS AND SAUCERS

500g white sugarpaste
pink food colour paste
blue food colour paste
yellow food colour paste
1 x Vanilla Shortbread dough
   (see page 186)
plain flour, to dust
5cm round cutter
icing sugar, to dust
1.4cm blossom cutter
100g bag white royal icing,
   no. 1 nozzle
48 large pastel-coloured
   marshmallows
48 Jazzies (chocolate drops with
   hundreds and thousands)

Toadstool Biscuits
VANILLA SHORTBREAD

Line two baking trays with baking parchment. Preheat the oven to 170°C/fan 160°C/340°F/gas mark 3½.

Roll out the dough on a floured work surface to 4mm thick and, using the toadstool template, cut out 40 toadstools. Place the biscuits on the trays and bake for eight to 10 minutes. Leave on the trays to cool.

For the red toadstools, colour 100g of the sugarpaste a deep red using both claret and Christmas red food colours (see page 168). Roll out to 2mm thick on a work surface dusted with icing sugar. Cut out 20 red toadstool caps using the template and stick them to the biscuits with royal icing. To make the polka dots, cut out white sugarpaste circles with the cutter or nozzle. Stick on with the royal icing. To decorate with sprinkles, pipe three or four caps at a time with royal icing. Tip the sprinkles on to a plate and press each biscuit into it.

✱ ALSO TRY WITH Chocolate Shortbread (see page 27)

MAKES 40

1 x Vanilla Shortbread dough
   (see page 186)
plain flour, to dust
7cm toadstool template

FOR THE RED TOADSTOOLS
150g white sugarpaste
claret food colour paste
Christmas red food colour paste
icing sugar, to dust
60g bag white royal icing,
   no. 1 nozzle
1 small round cutter or
   piping nozzle

FOR THE SPRINKLE TOADSTOOLS
hundreds and thousands

Cheshire Cat Fairy Cakes

ALL-IN-ONE LEMON CAKE

MAKES 30

FOR THE CAKES
30 purple fairy cake paper cases
1 x All-in-one Lemon Cake
   batter (see page 61)
juice of 1 lemon
5 tbsp caster sugar

TO ICE AND DECORATE
500g icing sugar, sifted, plus
   more if needed
7–8 tbsp lemon juice
grape violet food colour paste
400g white sugarpaste
yellow food colour paste
large circle cutter
very small circle cutter, or
   piping nozzle
60g bag white royal icing,
   no. 1 nozzle
20g bag black royal icing,
   no. 1 nozzle

'If I had a world of my own, everything would be nonsense. Nothing would be what it is because everything would be what it isn't. Any contrary-wise, what it is it wouldn't be, and what it wouldn't be, it would. You see?'
Alice in Wonderland, by Lewis Carroll

TO BAKE
Preheat the oven to 180°C/fan 170°C/350°F/gas mark 4. To bake the fairy cakes, line fairy cake tins with the paper cases, divide the batter between them and bake for 10–15 minutes, or until the cakes are well risen and spring back to the touch. (You may need to bake in two batches.) Meanwhile, make the syrup by mixing the lemon juice and sugar in a bowl. Immediately the cakes come from the oven, prick holes all over with a cocktail stick and douse each with a little syrup.

TO DECORATE
When ready to ice, place the icing sugar into a bowl and very gradually add enough lemon juice to make a pourable consistency. Stir in the violet food colour, a little at a time, as these colours are strong. If the icing has become too runny, thicken with a little more icing sugar; it should coat the back of a spoon. Pour on to the cakes and allow to dry.

To make the Cheshire cat face, divide the sugarpaste in half. Seal half of it in a polythene bag. Colour 100g yellow for the eyes and the remaining 100g the same purple as the glacé icing on the cakes for the ears and noses (see page 168). Keep all the colours sealed in separate polythene bags when not in use. To make the mouths, roll out the white sugarpaste to about 3mm thick and use the edge of the circle cutter to cut out 30 crescent moon shapes (each about 5cm long).

To make the eyes, roll out the yellow sugarpaste to about 3mm thick and use the end of a piping nozzle to make 60 eyes. Roll out the purple icing to about 3mm thick and cut out 60 triangles for the ears about 2cm long, scoring a line in the centre of each. Roll 30 tiny purple balls for the noses.

Using the white royal icing, stick all the eyes, ears, noses and mouths on to the cakes. Pipe on teeth with white royal icing, and whiskers and pupils with black royal icing.

✶ ALSO TRY WITH Liquorice Toffee Cupcakes (see page 160)

Fairies on Fairy Cakes

ALL-IN-ONE LEMON CAKE

Girls will love to share a party with fairies. The little tea set shown was given to my daughter from her grandfather.

TO BAKE

Preheat the oven to 180°C/fan 170°C/350°F/gas mark 4. Line two fairy cake tins with the cases and divide the batter between them. Bake for 15 minutes, or until they spring back to the touch. Mix the lemon juice and sugar in a bowl. While the cakes are hot, prick all over with a cocktail stick and douse with syrup. Leave to cool in the tins.

Place the icing sugar in a bowl and add just enough lemon juice to make a pourable consistency. Remove half to another bowl. Add a little pink colour to one bowl and a little yellow to the other to make pastel shades. Ice half the cakes pink and the other half yellow: pour a spoonful of the icing over each cake, gently easing it over with the back of a spoon so it spreads to the edges. Allow to set for an hour.

TO MAKE THE FAIRIES

Leave 100g of the sugarpaste white, colour 200g pale yellow (see page 168) and 200g a pale skin colour, with a pinprick each of pink and caramel-ivory food colours. Seal in polythene bags when not in use.

Take a piece of skin colour sugarpaste the size of a small cherry tomato. Roll into a ball and then make a cone. On a work surface dusted with icing sugar, roll out a little yellow sugarpaste about 2mm thick and, using the flower cutter, cut a 'dress'. Cut out a few tiny blossoms as well. Paint the tip of each cone with edible glue and place the dress over it, easing down and flaring it out. Roll a little ball from skin colour sugarpaste for the head. Glue the head on to the body and indent the eyes, using a cocktail stick, and the mouth, with the curve of a blossom cutter. Roll thin, 2cm- and 3cm-long sausages for the arms and legs. Using the glue and paint brush, stick the arms and legs to each body, under the dress. To make the wings, roll out the white sugarpaste to 2mm thick, and cut out butterflies. Lay on a sheet of paper and sprinkle with clear glitter, or paint the edges with glue and dip into gold glitter. Leave overnight. Cut out white blossoms.

Using royal icing, pipe on the hair and nose, then stick on a dragee tiara. Decorate each dress with blossoms – piping white centres – and dragees. Stick a fairy on each cake. Lightly sprinkle with clear glitter.

✱ ALSO TRY WITH All-in-one Chocolate Cake (see page 77)

MAKES 16–18

16–18 fairy cake paper cases
1 x All-in-one Lemon Cake
  batter (see page 61)

FOR THE SYRUP
juice of 1 lemon
5 tbsp caster sugar

FOR THE LEMON ICING
300g icing sugar, sifted
4–5 tbsp lemon juice
pink food colour paste
yellow food colour paste

TO MAKE 16 FAIRIES
500g white sugarpaste
caramel-ivory food colour paste
icing sugar, to dust
edible glue
edible clear glitter
edible gold glitter
60g bag white royal icing,
  no. 1 nozzle
selection of 2mm and 4mm
  dragees in gold and pink

SPECIAL EQUIPMENT
5cm flower cutter
tiny blossom cutter
small paint brush
4cm butterfly cutter

Rhubarb and Anise Crumble Cake

SERVES 12

FOR THE CAKE

240g unsalted butter, softened,
    plus more for the tin
240g self-raising flour
1 tsp baking powder
1 tsp salt
200g golden caster sugar
4 large eggs, lightly beaten
1 tsp vanilla extract
70ml crème fraîche
300g raw pink rhubarb, cut
    into pieces

FOR THE CRUMBLE TOPPING

3–4 tsp anise seeds (optional)
100g golden caster sugar
½ tsp salt
210g plain flour, sifted
160g unsalted butter, chilled
    and diced

FOR THE RHUBARB RIBBONS

vegetable oil (optional)
3 rhubarb stalks
6 tbsp caster sugar
3 tbsp apricot jam

Preheat the oven to 170°C/fan 160°C/340°F/gas mark 3½. Butter a 25cm round springform tin, and line the base with baking parchment.

Prepare the crumble topping. Place the anise seeds in a small pan over a moderate heat and toast very lightly, stirring a bit, to release the flavour. Grind to a powder in a mortar and pestle. Place the sugar, ground anise, salt and flour into a bowl. Rub in the butter until the mixture is of an even crumb consistency.

For the cake, sift the flour, baking powder and salt into a large bowl. Cream the butter and sugar for about five minutes until really light and fluffy. Add the eggs slowly, folding in a little of the flour. Next add the vanilla, fold in the remaining flour and the crème fraîche and, finally, stir in the rhubarb. Turn into the tin, sprinkle the crumble over and bake for 55–60 minutes, or until a skewer emerges clean. Leave in the tin on a wire rack for five minutes then turn out, crumble side up. Remove the papers and cool completely.

RHUBARB RIBBONS
Simpler to make than you think, and so professional.

Preheat the oven to very low (90°C/fan 80°C/195°F/gas mark ¼). If you have a sheet of re-usable cooking liner, place it on a baking tray (or lightly oil baking parchment, then wipe with kitchen paper, so only a very fine film of oil remains). With a very sharp knife, cut each rhubarb stalk lengthways into 2mm thick strips, then cut into 12–13cm lengths.

Place the sugar and 4 tbsp water into a very clean small pan over a low heat until the sugar dissolves. Boil for a minute or so, then cool. Dip in the rhubarb strips, shake off excess and lay them on the tray. Place in the oven for an hour, turn and cook for 30 minutes, or until they feel drier, though still slightly sticky. Remove to a wire rack. When cool and crisp, trim to shape with scissors. Store in very dry conditions, and use on the same or next day. Heat the jam gently, press through a sieve, and use it to stick the ribbons to the cake.

I love this cake, a version of a classic American coffee cake. Ring the changes with peaches or gooseberries, raspberries, cherries or blueberries. I've used the young, pink rhubarb stalks that are harvested by candlelight in Yorkshire and available in early spring. Serve with vanilla-flavoured crème fraîche or mascarpone (mix in the seeds of a vanilla pod or 1 tsp vanilla extract).

Piggy Bank
VICTORIA SPONGE

I just love this spotty piggy bank; make it in any colour of your choice. Don't think this is a cake just for children, adults fall for its charm too…

TO BAKE
Preheat the oven to 180°C/fan 170°C/350°F/gas mark 4.

Butter the cake tin very well indeed. Place a piece of baking parchment over the hole in the base of one of the semi-spherical halves. Make a stand of twisted aluminium foil to stop the tin from rolling around in the oven, and stand the other on the base supplied.

For this all-in-one sponge, use either an electric mixer and beater attachment, a bowl and hand-held electric whisk, or a food processor.

Sift the flour and baking powder into the bowl, add the butter, eggs, sugar and vanilla. Beat together until well mixed (taking care not to over-mix) and divide the batter between the prepared tins. Bake for 40–45 minutes, or until a skewer emerges clean.

Remove from the oven, leave for a couple of minutes, then run a knife around the rim of each tin and turn the cake out on to a wire rack. Cool completely.

Meanwhile, to make the buttercream, in an electric mixer (or in a bowl using a hand-held whisk) beat the butter until really pale and fluffy, then add the vanilla extract. Add the icing sugar and beat for at least five minutes until really creamy.

SERVES 20

FOR THE VICTORIA SPONGE
280g unsalted butter, really soft, diced, plus more for the tin
280g self-raising flour
1½ tsp baking powder
5 eggs, lightly beaten
280g golden caster sugar
1 tsp vanilla extract

FOR THE BUTTERCREAM
250g unsalted butter, softened
1 tsp vanilla extract
250g icing sugar, sifted

SPECIAL EQUIPMENT
2-litre spherical cake tin (see suppliers, page 188)

continued…

4 tbsp lemon curd, or strawberry
   or raspberry jam
1kg ready-mixed pink sugarpaste
icing sugar, to dust
60g bag white royal icing,
   no. 1 nozzle
1 packet white chocolate buttons
1 bag gold chocolate coins (or
   more, to surround the cake)

SPECIAL EQUIPMENT
15cm round thin cake card, cut
   down to a 12cm round
paint brush
30cm round cake drum

TO ASSEMBLE AND DECORATE

Cut a small amount of cake from the base of one of the two halves to stop it from rolling around. Trim the tops flat, if necessary, and then cut each in half horizontally, to make four layers. Stick the base cake to the thin cake board with a little buttercream. Sandwich the layers together with the buttercream and a layer of the lemon curd or jam. Use the remaining buttercream to cover the entire ball. Place the cake on a large work surface.

Knead the sugarpaste on a clean board dusted with icing sugar. Once it is malleable, roll it out into a large circle 35–40cm in diameter and 5–6mm thick. Loosely wrap around the rolling pin (or lift with your hands) and place centrally over the cake. Ease around the cake, rubbing with your hands and smoothing away creases or imperfections. Press down and in around the base. Cut away excess, removing and discarding any pieces that have buttercream on them. You can use the remaining sugarpaste (re-seal it in a polythene bag).

While the sugarpaste is still soft, use the end of the paint brush to make a 6cm-long coin slot along the top of the cake. Make two little holes for the eyes and one hole at the other end to insert the tail. Leave the sugarpaste to set for a few hours, if you can.

To make the ears, simply roll out a piece of the leftover sugarpaste to about 3mm thick and cut two triangles, each about 5x5x5cm. Curl them at the tips. To make the tail, roll a sausage of sugarpaste about 10cm long and 5mm wide. Roll around the handle of a wooden spoon and leave to dry for a few hours, or overnight. To make the snout, roll a piece of sugarpaste into a ball about 3cm wide, flatten and make two holes on the surface of one flat side with the end of the paint brush. Make the legs by rolling four slightly smaller flattened balls of sugarpaste in the same way. Stick the ears, snout and tail to the pig with royal icing and stick the chocolate buttons all over the cake.

Place an upturned saucer into the centre of the cake drum. Stand the pig on top and half-tuck his legs under his body, securing with royal icing. Leave to dry, then remove the saucer. Finish the cake by sticking a chocolate coin into the slot on the back and scattering the remaining coins all around.

✱ ALSO TRY WITH Banoffee Cake (see page 42), or All-in-one Chocolate Cake (see page 77), or Madeira Cake (see page 99)

Blackberry, Lavender, Rose and White Chocolate Cake

Sharply intense blackberries cut the sweetness of white chocolate. Try to use wild berries in season, or cultivated if necessary, or use raspberries. All parts of this cake can be made a day before and assembled on the day.

Preheat the oven to 180°C/fan 170°C/350°F/gas mark 4. Butter two 20cm round sandwich tins and line the bases with baking parchment.

Melt the chocolate, butter and milk in a bowl set over simmering water, making sure the bowl does not touch the water. Leave to cool.

Meanwhile, in a large bowl, sift together the flour and baking powder. Beat in the sugar, eggs and vanilla and lastly the slightly cooled chocolate mixture. Divide the batter between the tins and bake for 35–40 minutes, or until a skewer emerges clean.

Remove from the oven, leave for a minute or two, then run a knife around the rim to loosen the cakes from the tin and turn out on to a wire rack. Remove the papers and leave until completely cold.

For the ganache, place the chocolate in a bowl. Bring the cream and rose water to a boil in a pan and pour over the chocolate. Leave for a few seconds, then stir until smooth. Once cold, chill well in the fridge, then whisk until thickened.

For the compote, heat the lemon juice, lavender heads, sugar and blackberries together very gently until the sugar dissolves, the fruit juices start running and everything comes together. Leave for a few hours, or preferably overnight, to allow the flavours to mingle. Remove any excess liquid if necessary, as it will spoil the finished cake, and remove the lavender.

To assemble, place one tier of the cake on a serving plate or cake stand, spread it with some of the ganache and all of the blackberry compote. Place the other cake on top and spread the rest of the ganache around the sides and top. Decorate with rose petals, or sprigs of lavender, or even a few full-blown roses.

SERVES 10

FOR THE CAKE
180g unsalted butter, diced, plus more for the tins
200g Swiss white chocolate, broken into pieces
200ml whole milk
280g self-raising flour
1 tsp baking powder
250g golden caster sugar
3 eggs, lightly beaten
1 tsp vanilla extract

FOR THE WHITE CHOCOLATE GANACHE
200g Swiss white chocolate, finely chopped
200ml double cream
2–3 tsp rose water (add little by little to your taste)

FOR THE COMPOTE
juice of ½ large lemon
3–4 heads fresh (or dried) lavender
150g golden caster sugar
300g blackberries

TO DECORATE
rose petals
sprigs of fresh lavender (optional)
a few full-blown roses (optional)

Angel Surprise Cake
ANGEL CAKE

SERVES 10

FOR THE CAKE
225g icing sugar, sifted twice
140g plain flour, sifted twice
10 egg whites, at room
    temperature
½ tsp salt
1½ tsp cream of tartar
finely grated zest of 1 unwaxed
    lemon (or orange)
1 tsp vanilla extract
pink food colour paste
orange food colour paste

FOR THE FROSTING
180g white caster sugar
1 egg white
2 tbsp lemon juice (or orange)
½ tsp cream of tartar
pinch of salt
50g white marshmallows,
    chopped
1 tsp vanilla extract

SPECIAL EQUIPMENT
angel cake tin (optional)
30cm cake drum (optional)

TO DECORATE
everlasting flowers (see page 117)

I made this for my teenage daughter's recent birthday and everyone shrieked with delight when she cut into it. The sweet cake (popular in the United States) contains no fat, so needs to be eaten on the day.

Preheat the oven to 160°C/fan 150°C/325°F/gas mark 3. Use a 23cm springform cake tin, or angel cake tin; there is no need to butter it. Place the icing sugar in one bowl and the flour in another.

In a large, clean, degreased bowl (wipe the bowl first with half a cut lemon and dry with kitchen paper), whisk the egg whites until frothy and foamy (I used a hand-held electric whisk). Add the salt and cream of tartar and continue to whisk to soft peaks. Sprinkle over the icing sugar, 2 tbsp at a time, whisking after each addition. It is fatal to this cake to over-whisk, as you need to keep it very light. Lastly, add the lemon zest and vanilla. Fold in the flour 2 tbsp at a time with a large metal spoon until you have a light, airy cake batter.

Divide into three. Colour one part deep pink, the second a lighter pink and the last pale orange. Do this very gently and do not be too enthusiastic when mixing the batter, as you don't want to beat out all the air you have just whisked in. If the colour is not completely folded in and is marbled, that is fine. Spoon each into the tin, to achieve layers of colours. Very gently tap the tin on a work surface to remove air bubbles. Bake for 35–40 minutes, or until the cake springs back to the touch and has a beautiful golden crust. Remove from the oven and cool the cake upside down with the tin over it. I placed the hole of the angel cake tin on the neck of a wine bottle, propped against the wall.

To make the frosting, put the sugar, egg white, lemon juice, cream of tartar and salt in a heatproof bowl, and fit it over a pan of very, very gently simmering water; it mustn't boil. Once melted, stir in the marshmallows and vanilla and stir until smooth and glossy. Keep the bowl over the heat and, with an electric whisk (don't even think about doing this with a hand-held whisk) whisk for about five minutes, or until the frosting has increased in volume, is thick and shiny and forms soft peaks. Remove from the heat and use straight away.

Loosen the sides and centre of the cake by running a knife around the rims and turn the cake on to the drum or serving plate. Spread the frosting all over with a palette knife (if baked in an angel cake tin, into the hole too). Allow to set for an hour or so before adding the flowers.

continued...

Everlasting Flowers

Do use crêpe paper in colours of your choice; each sheet should measure 20x50cm. These are the colours I used.

TO MAKE A PINK ROSE

First of all take the darker pink paper and cut out four x 8cm squares. Scrunch two up to make a tear drop shape, take a third square, place it over the fattest end of the tear drop and gather it at the base. Wrap the end of a length of wire firmly around the base. Fold the final square diagonally in half to make a triangle and fold the long side around the rest quite tightly; this is the central bud.

Next cut out all the petals. When cutting out the petals, it is much easier to fold the paper over a few times, trace the template of a petal on to the top layer and cut through. I cut out two small petals in darker pink. Then, from the pale pink paper, I cut three small and seven large petals. Try to give the petals a bit of movement, either by running your finger from the base to the top, or curling the tips around a pencil or pen, so that they aren't completely flat.

Start with the two darker smaller petals and wrap around the bud, overlapping slightly. Tweak into position and secure firmly with sticky tape. Continue with the three small pale pink petals and then the seven larger, using sticky tape to secure at the base. Finally conceal all the sticky tape by wrapping florist's tape around the base, as tightly as you can. I also made roses in orange.

TO MAKE A CARNATION

Cut several long strips of yellow crêpe paper about 24cm long and 4.5cm wide. You will need four lengths of darker yellow and four of paler yellow for one carnation. Fold the strips into four, keeping them as one length. Using pinking shears, cut a frilly pattern along the top edge. If you don't have these scissors simply cut a very fine zigzag along one length to form the frilly edge of the carnation. Wrap a dark yellow strip around to form the centre of the flower and secure with wire. Continue to wind around the other pieces of darker yellow, then the paler yellow pieces.

Frill and tweak out the petals with your fingers. Place the sugarpaste, if using, in the central hole of the angel cake. Twist the wires of the flowers to make a bunch and insert into the centre of the cake. If you've made the cake in a springform cake tin, lay the flowers on top.

1 sheet dark pink crêpe paper
green medium-thick florist's wire
(25cm per flower)
1 sheet pale pink crêpe paper
sticky tape
green florist's tape
1 sheet pale orange crêpe paper
1 sheet dark yellow crêpe paper
1 sheet pale yellow crêpe paper
pinking shears or zigzag craft
scissors (optional)
40g sugarpaste (optional)

SMALL PETAL

LARGE PETAL

Marzipan Fruits Hat

EASIEST EVER ALL-IN-ONE FRUIT CAKE

SERVES 10

FOR THE HAT
1.5kg white sugarpaste
grape violet food colour paste
icing sugar, to dust
1 x Easiest Ever All-in-one 15cm
    round fruit cake (see page 186)
3 tbsp apricot jam
60g bag purple royal icing
60cm 5cm-wide black grosgrain
    ribbon
black feathers
black netting
sticky tape
135cm 1.5cm-wide black satin
    ribbon, for the board

SPECIAL EQUIPMENT
40cm round cake drum
15cm round cake drum

A sensational centrepiece. Don't be put off if making sugar roses and fruits is not for you. Exquisite ribbons, feathers, flowers, butterflies and birds can be found easily: go and raid the local haberdasher's. Then you only have to bake the cake, cover it and the board with sugarpaste and decorate! The roses can be made with sugarpaste, which is easier to handle than petal paste (see suppliers, p188), though the petals will be less fine.

TO ASSEMBLE

As usual, all sugar decorations may be made weeks in advance and stored in a cardboard box. Begin by colouring the sugarpaste deep purple, using the grape violet food colour (see page 168). If you can, leave overnight as it will become much more manageable.

To cover the large cake drum, dust it lightly with icing sugar and flick a little water over it to act as a glue. On a clean work surface lightly dusted with icing sugar, roll out 1kg of the purple sugarpaste to a rough circle slightly larger than the 40cm drum and about 5mm thick. Roll loosely around the rolling pin on to the drum. Rub down on the drum with your hands and cut away excess all around the board.

Cut the top surface from the fruit cake at a slight angle, so that one side is a centimetre or so higher. Turn the cake upside down. Place the 15cm drum on the work surface. Warm the apricot jam, push it through a sieve if necessary, and brush a little on to the drum. Place the cake on to it and brush the remaining jam over the top and sides.

On a clean work surface lightly dusted with icing sugar, roll out the remaining purple sugarpaste into a rough circle slightly larger than the top and sides of the cake and about 5mm thick. Roll loosely around the rolling pin and place on to the cake, rubbing and pressing the icing with your hands, then cut away excess around the edges. Spread some purple royal icing into the centre of the large cake drum and place the covered cake centrally on to it. It is best to allow the sugarpaste to dry for at least a couple of hours and preferably overnight. Decorate with your ribbons, feathers and netting – or other selected decorations – using the purple icing and sticky tape to attach.

TO MAKE THE FRUIT

Should you decide to make the sugar fruits and flowers, here is how I made mine. Make up all the coloured icing, using the combinations given right (see page 168).

To make the pears, remove a tiny piece of sugarpaste for the stalks. Mould the pears: make two balls, form each into a cone and model the stalk end slightly narrower. Indent the top slightly and leave overnight. Then mix a little caramel-ivory colour with water, dip in a paint brush and flick it – from quite close – over the pears.

To make the orange, simply make a ball of the coloured sugarpaste by rolling it in your hands. Roll over a fine grater to make the mottled skin. Allow to dry, preferably overnight. Make the clementines and the lemon in exactly the same way, moulding the lemon shape, and pressing a clove into the top of each clementine. If you wish, spray the lemon, orange and clementines with the glaze spray for a shine.

To make the cut fruits, cut one pear, the orange, the lemon and one clementine in half. (This is best done after they have dried overnight.) Re-shape slightly if necessary. On a clean work surface lightly dusted with icing sugar, roll out the very pale cream sugarpaste as thin as you can. One by one, brush each cut side of the fruits with a little edible glue, lay the cream sugarpaste on to it and cut to shape with a sharp craft knife. Allow to dry for at least 30 minutes. To paint, use a very fine paint brush and a palette of most of the food colours listed. As always, if you paint from real fruits, they will be more realistic.

TO MAKE SUGARPASTE ROSES

Make up the coloured icing, using the combinations given right (see page 168), making half of each batch in a darker tone. Take 25g of each tone of the paste for each rose. Split a polythene bag open and place on a work surface. Take about one-third of the darker colour, roll into a ball and then a cone. Flatten the base on the work surface and indent into a cone on top of a rough ball.

Using half the darker colour, roll three balls and lay them on one side of the bag. Fold over the other side and flatten each ball until quite thin. Keep one side of each petal slightly thicker (to go around the cone centre). Peel back the bag gently. Take one petal at a time and, with the thinner part uppermost, mould it around the cone, completely covering the top. Take the second petal and place it centrally over the seam of the first (again thinner side uppermost) and mould it around the cone. Place the third petal directly opposite. Tweak the petals as you work, to look like a real rose. Make three more darker-toned petals in the same way, each overlapping the last, and tweaking the petals as you work. Take half the lighter toned paste, make a row of five petals and lastly – using up the remaining paste – a final row of five petals. With a knife, cut away the base at an angle.

✱ ALSO TRY WITH Coffee Cake (see page 155)

FOR THE FRUIT AND ROSES

FOR TWO PEARS
120g white sugarpaste
caramel-ivory food colour paste
Christmas green food colour paste
primrose food colour paste
paint brush

FOR ONE ORANGE
50g white sugarpaste
peach food colour paste
egg yellow food colour paste
dot of claret food colour paste

FOR THREE CLEMENTINES
60g white sugarpaste
peach food colour paste
primrose food colour paste
dot of claret food colour paste
3 cloves

FOR ONE LEMON
30g white sugarpaste
primrose food colour paste
edible glaze spray (optional)

FOR THE CUT EDGES OF THE FRUIT
30g white sugarpaste
primrose food colour paste
edible glue

FOR ONE DARK RED ROSE
50g white petal paste
claret food colour paste
Christmas red food colour paste

FOR THREE PINK ROSES
150g white petal paste
claret food colour paste

FOR TWO ORANGE ROSES
100g white petal paste
peach food colour paste
egg yellow food colour paste
claret food colour paste

Pastel Ice Cream Sandwiches

To make the little biscuits, divide the dough into three and, on a board dusted with flour, roll it out thinly to about 2mm thick. Using the round cutter, cut out the biscuits and layer them up between sheets of silicone paper in an airtight container. Re-roll the dough until you have 30. Repeat with the rest of the dough until you have 90 biscuits. You can freeze them now, and bake later, or lay them on a couple of baking trays lined with baking parchment.

To bake, preheat the oven to 170°C/fan 160°C/340°F/gas mark 3½ and place the trays in the oven for eight to 10 minutes. They are rolled quite finely, so don't take long to cook.

The ice cream can be made in advance too. It is best eaten within a couple of days, but can be kept for two or three weeks.

Split the vanilla pod lengthways and, with the tip of a knife, scrape out the seeds and reserve. Place the cream and pod in a pan and bring to a boil. Meanwhile, in a large bowl with a hand-held whisk, or in an electric mixer, whisk the egg yolks and sugar for a good three to four minutes until really thick and creamy, and add the salt. Remove the vanilla pod from the cream. Then, very slowly, (whisking as you pour) add the hot cream mixture to the eggs. Pass through a sieve, add the vanilla seeds and allow to cool.

Add sugar and lemon juice to taste to all three fruit purées. Divide the ice cream base into three equal parts, and place each into a tray. Stir a different fruit purée into each. Cover the trays with lids and freeze for two hours. Remove, whisk with an electric whisk and refreeze. Repeat twice more. Alternatively, churn each flavour in an ice cream machine, then freeze in the trays.

When set, cut 15 circles from each ice cream flavour with the round cutter. Place the discs on a tray and return to the freezer. Reform the offcuts of ice cream and freeze.

To serve, sandwich an ice cream disc between two biscuits and dust with icing sugar, if you like.

✴ ALSO TRY WITH Chocolate Shortbread (see page 27)

MAKES 45

FOR THE BISCUITS
1 x Vanilla Shortbread dough
 (see page 186)
plain flour, to dust
icing sugar, to dust (optional)

FOR THE ICE CREAM BASE
1 vanilla pod
500ml double cream
3 egg yolks, at room temperature
150g caster or vanilla sugar
pinch of sea salt

FOR THE ICE CREAM FLAVOURINGS
caster sugar, to taste
lemon juice, to taste
150g strawberry purée
150g Alphonso mango purée
 (canned, if not in season)
150g blackcurrant purée

SPECIAL EQUIPMENT
4.3cm round cutter
3 identical trays; I used 23x18cm
 foil casserole containers

Make a stash of these and whisk them out of the freezer at any children's party. I have made the ice cream and shortbread, but you could cheat and buy 90 biscuits and 1 litre of good-quality ice cream. Try flavouring the ice cream with cocoa powder, fruit purée, or small chocolate chips. No need for an ice cream machine if you don't have one.

Bejewelled Elephant
MASALA CHAI CAKE

SERVES 12

TO DECORATE
1.4kg white sugarpaste
egg yellow food colour paste
black food colour paste
claret food colour paste
1 x Masala Chai Cake, baked in a
    20cm round tin (see page 184)
1 x Ginger Fudge Frosting recipe
    (see page 184)
icing sugar, to dust
edible glue (optional)
60g bag white royal icing,
    no. 1 nozzle
selection of 2mm and 4mm gold
    and green dragees
clear piping gel
Christmas red food colour paste
mint green food colour paste
royal gold powder
a little clear spirit, such as vodka
70cm (5–6cm wide) bejewelled
    or bright ribbon

SPECIAL EQUIPMENT
25cm round gold cake drum
    (optional)
elephant template (see opposite)
sharp craft knife
small paint brush

TO DECORATE

Colour 1kg of the sugarpaste a strong yellow-orange with egg yellow food colour, 200g elephant grey, using the black, and 100g two shades of pink, using the claret (see page 168). Leave the rest white. Trim the cake level, turn it upside down and adhere it to the cake drum, if using, or a cake stand with a little of the frosting. Spread the remaining frosting over the whole cake and sides.

Make the tusk: roll a thin sausage of white sugarpaste to 5cm long, tapering at one end. Dust a work surface with icing sugar. Knead the orange sugarpaste until pliable and roll out to 5mm thick and slightly larger than the cake and sides. Place it over the cake. Smooth gently with your hands, cut away the excess and reserve. Leave overnight.

For the elephant, on a work surface dusted with icing sugar, roll out the grey sugarpaste to 4mm thick and slightly larger than the template. Place the template over the sugarpaste and, using a craft knife, cut out the elephant. Lift on to the cake and, either with edible glue or royal icing, stick it to the top of the cake. Cut out one grey ear too. Roll out the deep pink sugarpaste to 4mm thick and 9cm square. Cut zigzags at the base and stick on the elephant's back. Roll out a smaller piece and cut out the cap. Stick to the head. With a knife, score a criss-cross and press in tiny gold dragees. Roll out the orange sugarpaste to 9cm wide and 1cm shorter than the deep pink square. Cut zigzags at the base and stick on top. Repeat with the paler pink sugarpaste.

Pipe three rows of little flowers on the cloth. Once dry, place green dragees in the centre of one row. Mix clear piping gel with Christmas red food colour and, using a paint brush, make a ruby centre for the other two rows and the base of the orange cloth. Make an emerald for his forehead with clear piping gel and mint green food colour and pipe white dots around it. Allow the dots to dry for an hour then, with a fine brush, paint with the gold powder mixed with vodka. Mould 1.5cm tassels from the pink and orange sugarpaste. Mould the ropes for his feet by twisting long thin sausages of orange and deeper pink.

Brush the orange cloth with edible glue, or royal icing, and sprinkle over the tiny dragees. Using royal icing or edible glue, attach a gold dragee eye, the ear and the tusk, then pipe on the nails. Finally, attach the tassels, ropes and ribbon (seam at the back).

✚ ALSO TRY WITH Banoffee Cake (see page 42)

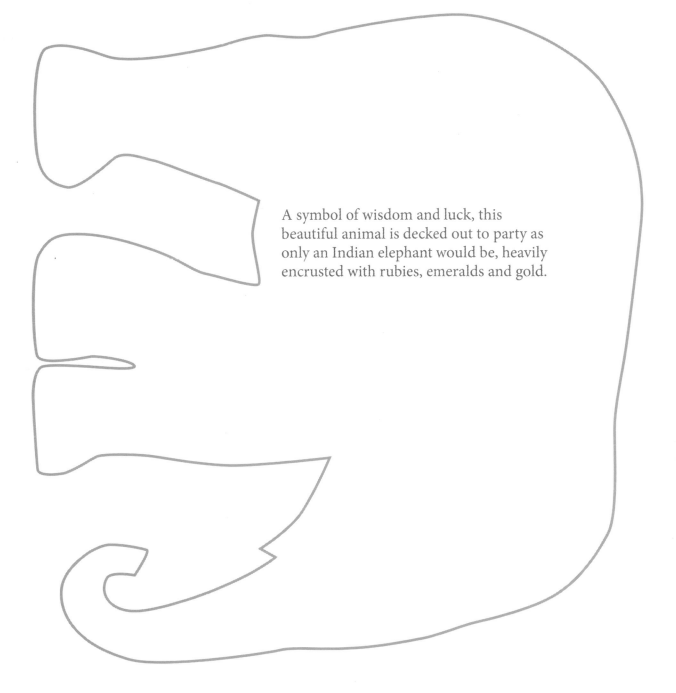

A symbol of wisdom and luck, this beautiful animal is decked out to party as only an Indian elephant would be, heavily encrusted with rubies, emeralds and gold.

A Fantasy Castle

TOFFEE CAKE

Perfect for any little princess!

TO DECORATE

Cover the 30cm round drum a day before. On a work surface dusted with icing sugar, roll out 1kg of sugarpaste to a circle larger than the drum and about 5mm thick. Sprinkle the drum with icing sugar and flick over a little water. Loosely roll the sugarpaste around the rolling pin and lift on to the drum. Rub with your hands. Cut away excess and reserve. Roll sausages of sugarpaste for the five turrets, and cut to size. My tallest was 6cm, and they ranged from 3–3.5cm wide. Dry flat, rolling now and again so there is no flat side. Cover the cones with royal icing and roll in sparkling sugar. Stand upright to dry.

If necessary, trim the cakes level. Turn flat side up and sandwich the two 20cm cakes with buttercream. Split the 15cm cake in half and spread buttercream in the centre. Spread the remaining buttercream all over both cakes. Using royal icing, adhere the 20cm cake to the 20cm board, and the 15cm cake to the 15cm drum. Next, cover both cakes with sugarpaste, one at a time: on a work surface dusted with icing sugar, roll out two circles slightly larger than each cake and sides, about 5mm thick, roll loosely around your rolling pin and lift on to the cake. Rub over the top and sides until smooth.

Adhere the large cake to the 30cm drum with royal icing. Spread royal icing on top and place on the top tier. Insert a dowel into each turret. Spread the bases with royal icing and push four into the top tier, sticking the fifth to the drum. The dowelling is higher than the top of each turret, but helps to support the cake; trim as necessary. Stick the ice cream cones to the turrets. To make the ramparts, roll out 22x2cm strips of sugarpaste, each 5mm thick. Cut out squares along one long side. Stick on the ramparts with royal icing. Next, stick sugar cubes to the edges of the cakes with royal icing, attach dragees to the ramparts and a sugar pearl to each sugar cube. Using the icing glitter tube, (or no. 1 nozzle and royal icing), pipe windows, door and flower stems. Roll a piece of sugarpaste to 2mm thick, cut out 30–40 blossoms and adhere to the stems. Finish with a piped centre. Make five ribbon flags, tape to cocktail sticks and insert into the cones. Tape the fluffy ribbon around the base.

★ ALSO TRY WITH Victoria Sponge (see page 109)

SERVES 15

FOR THE CAKE
1 x Toffee Cake (see page 187)
2 x Toffee Buttercream recipe
   (see page 42)

SPECIAL EQUIPMENT
30cm round cake drum
20cm round cake board
15cm round cake drum
5 dowelling rods, or wooden
   skewers
13mm blossom cutter

TO DECORATE
icing sugar, to dust
2.35kg white sugarpaste
5 pointed ice cream cones
400g white royal icing
1 bottle white sparkling sugar
   (or granulated sugar)
piping bag, no. 1 nozzle
55 white sugar cubes
4mm dragees, in mixed colours
pearlised sugar pearls
white glitter writing icing tube
40cm 5mm-wide pink gingham
   ribbon
double-sided sticky tape
1 metre fluffy white or pink
   ribbon

Blueberry Yogurt Fairy Cakes

MAKES 36

FOR THE CAKES
36 paper fairy cake cases
300g self-raising flour
1 tsp baking powder
½ tsp salt
220g plain yogurt, at room
    temperature
2 eggs, lightly beaten
170g golden caster sugar
125g unsalted butter, melted
    and cooled
200g blueberries
1 tsp vanilla extract
finely grated zest of 1 unwaxed
    lemon

FOR THE TOPPING
600g cream cheese (half-fat, if
    you prefer)
120g golden icing sugar, sifted
grape violet food colour paste

TO DECORATE
250g blueberries
3 tbsp caster sugar
squeeze of lemon juice

Preheat the oven to 170°C/fan 160°C/340°F/gas mark 3½.

Line fairy cake trays with the paper cases. Sift together the flour, baking powder and salt. In a large bowl, mix the yogurt, eggs, sugar and butter using a large spoon. Add the flour mixture, berries, vanilla and lemon zest. Stir until combined, but do not over-mix. Divide between the cases and bake for 12–15 minutes, or until the cakes spring back to the touch. (You may need to bake in batches.) Stand for a few minutes in the trays, then remove to cool on a wire rack.

To make the topping, beat together the cream cheese and icing sugar. Add enough food colour to make a pale lilac. Divide the cream cheese between the cakes.

For the decoration, place the blueberries in a pan with the sugar, lemon juice and 1 tbsp water. Very lightly stew together for a minute or two, then strain the blueberries and dry on kitchen towel. Reduce the blueberry syrup in the pan until quite sticky and, when cool, swirl a little on to the frosting on each cake using the back of a spoon. Just before serving, place about three of the blueberries on each cake.

(If you do not wish to poach the blueberries and drizzle over the syrup, then simply top each cake with a few uncooked blueberries.)

These delicious cakes, oozing with blueberries, will convince even the most health-conscious that eating cake can be a fairly wholesome experience! Ring the changes by using raspberries or blackberries, or a mixture.

Spun Sugar Pile

LIQUORICE TOFFEE CAKE

SERVES 10

FOR THE CAKE
85g unsalted butter, softened, plus more for the tins
100ml whole milk
30g liquorice (I used 22 x 6.5cm lengths of soft, sweet Australian liquorice), roughly chopped
200g dates, pitted and chopped
175g self-raising flour
1 tsp bicarbonate of soda
140g golden caster sugar
seeds of 1 vanilla pod, or 1 tsp vanilla extract
2 eggs, lightly beaten

FOR THE BUTTERCREAM
1½ x Liquorice Caramel Buttercream recipe (see page 160)

SPECIAL EQUIPMENT
20cm round cake board or cake stand

A nest of very finely spun sugar on top of a cake is a real showstopper. Once mastered, it is a relatively quick, easy and inexpensive way to decorate a cake. However, it needs a little patience and it is essential to follow the instructions very carefully. Caramelised sugar reaches a temperature higher than boiling water and, if not treated with respect, can be very dangerous. Don't try to do this with young children around! The spun sugar should keep for a few hours in a dry place. Keep it out of a steamy kitchen and away from all moisture; damp weather won't help at all.

TO BAKE
Preheat the oven to 180°C/fan 170°C/350°F/gas mark 4. Butter two 15cm, 7.5cm deep round cake tins and line the bases with baking parchment. In a small saucepan, bring the milk and liquorice to a boil. Remove from the heat, stir and press on the liquorice to extract the flavour. Cover and leave to infuse for at least 30 minutes. Taste; the milk should be a 'liquorice milk', then strain. Meanwhile, in a heatproof bowl, pour 175ml boiling water over the dates and leave to soak for 20 minutes, then mash with a fork.

Sift the flour and bicarbonate of soda into a bowl. Cream together the butter, sugar and vanilla seeds (or extract) for about five minutes in an electric mixer. Add the eggs gradually, with 1 tbsp flour to stop the mixture curdling. Fold in the remaining flour, date mixture and milk. Divide the batter between the tins and bake for 30–35 minutes, or until a skewer emerges clean. Leave in the tins for a minute or two, then turn out on to a wire rack to cool completely. Remove the papers. Trim the tops level, if necessary.

To ice the cake, place one cake on to your board or cake stand and spread the top with a layer of the buttercream. Place the other half on top, flat side up. Spread the remaining buttercream all over the top and sides and smooth with a palette knife.

FOR THE SPUN SUGAR

Have to hand a small bowl of cold water, a large bowl of cold water, and baking parchment laid over a rolling pin.

Place the sugar and 225ml water into the pan and, on a low heat, allow all the sugar to dissolve, stirring a little with a metal spoon. Use the brush dipped in water to wipe away any sugar crystals around the side. You must make sure you can't see any sugar granules in the pan before you turn up the heat to high and bring to a boil. The caramel will rise in temperature to 155°C! It is possible to make this without a sugar thermometer, you just need to learn to recognise exactly when to remove the pan from the heat... not too soon or too late. It turns quickly from a perfect golden molten liquid to a pan of burnt sugar!

When you boil the caramel hard, it will go through various stages. The caramel will turn to a beautiful light golden colour. Test it by dropping a small piece into the small bowl of cold water. If it forms a ball, snaps and crackles, it is ready.

Remove from the heat and plunge the pan into the large bowl of water to stop it cooking. Hold the sawn-off whisk (or the 2 forks back to back), dip into the caramel and flick backwards and forwards over the rolling pin. The caramel strands will dry very quickly. Loosely gather up and mould the strands to suit the top of the cake.

When ready to serve the cake, take the spun sugar and cup loosely in your hands. Press ever so gently to form a ball and place on top.

A quite stunning cake for any age!

HOW TO CLEAN A CARAMEL PAN

Fill the pan with water and boil until all the caramel has dissolved. Then clean the pan as usual.

✶ ALSO TRY WITH Banoffee Cake (see page 42)

FOR THE SPUN SUGAR PILE
225g caster sugar

SPECIAL EQUIPMENT
meticulously clean copper, or
    heavy-based, small pan
pastry brush
sugar thermometer (optional)
sawn-off whisk, or 2 forks

Merry-Go-Round
RAINBOW VICTORIA SPONGE

SERVES 12

FOR THE CAKE
225g unsalted butter, really soft,
    diced, plus more for the tins
red food colour paste
orange food colour paste
yellow food colour paste
green food colour paste
blue food colour paste
purple food colour paste
225g self-raising flour
1 tsp baking powder
4 eggs, lightly beaten
225g golden caster sugar
1 tsp vanilla extract

FOR THE BUTTERCREAM
250g unsalted butter, softened
250g icing sugar, sifted
1 tsp vanilla extract

All the fun of the fair! Every single crumb of this cake is really colourful, as I've turned the Victoria sponge into a rainbow cake. If you feel you would rather make a plain sponge, simply omit the colouring. The poles and horses need to be made a day or so ahead; stick the horses on to the poles the day before too.

TO BAKE
Preheat the oven to 180°C/fan 170°C/350°F/gas mark 4. Butter two 20cm round sandwich tins and line the bases with baking parchment. Have ready six little bowls, six cocktail sticks and six teaspoons, and all the food colour paste pots open.

I use an electric mixer and beater attachment to make this, but you could use a food processor, or a bowl and hand-held whisk. Sift the flour and baking powder into the bowl, add the butter, eggs, sugar and vanilla. Beat until well blended, but don't over-mix.

Now, divide the batter between the six bowls and add enough food colour to each to make a red, orange, yellow, green, blue and purple. This may seem complicated, but it isn't. Place the cake batter in one cake tin at a time. Start by dolloping two-thirds of the red right into the centre of one tin. Next take a little less of the orange and place in the centre on top of the red, then the yellow, green, blue and finally purple, which is the smallest amount. There is no need to swirl the colours together... just believe me! The batter should spread to the edges of the tins when baked, but you can spread it very slightly now, if you wish. Repeat with the second tin, but this time start with the remaining purple cake batter, the remaining blue, green, yellow, orange and finally the red in the centre which is the smallest amount. You now have two tins with the rainbow colours in reverse.

Bake for 20–25 minutes, or until a skewer emerges clean. Remove from the oven, and after a couple of minutes run a knife around the rim of each cake and turn them out on to a wire rack. Remove the papers and leave to cool completely.

Meanwhile, make the buttercream. Beat the butter with an electric whisk for up to five minutes, until really pale. Add the icing sugar and vanilla and beat for another five minutes, until really light and fluffy.

TO DECORATE

Set aside 250g sugarpaste, and colour the rest deep lilac (see page 168). When the cakes are cold, level the tops. Take the 20cm cake board, spread on a little buttercream and place one of the cakes on to it. Spread buttercream on the top and place on the other cake, flat side up. Cover the top and sides with the remaining buttercream.

On a work surface dusted with icing sugar, take half the lilac sugarpaste and roll out to 30cm round and 5mm thick. Roll loosely around the rolling pin and ease over the cake. Rub with your hands until smooth, and cut off the excess. Any remaining clean sugarpaste can be stored with the rest of the lilac sugarpaste. Mix in more of the lilac food colour, to cover the board and make the lilac diamonds. Dust the 30cm drum with icing sugar and sprinkle with water. On a work surface dusted with icing sugar, roll out the deep lilac sugarpaste to 3mm thick and larger than the drum. Wrap around the rolling pin and lift on to the drum. Smooth, and trim the excess. (Cut stars from the offcuts as well as from tiny pieces of sugarpaste in different colours; reserve the rest.) Roll out the white sugarpaste to 5mm thick. Cut out eight horses. Stick a dragee eye on each with royal icing.

Cut the dowelling rods and stick of rock to 19cm long. Wind 60cm ribbon around each pole, securing with tape and stopping where the pole goes into the cake. The poles support the dome, so make sure they are level! Stick the horses to the poles at different heights with royal icing. Stick ribbon bows and sugarpaste stars on the horses and dry flat. To assemble, place the rock in the centre of the cake and the poles all around. Cut a slit to the centre of the cardboard circle, make a dome, and tape the seam. Using tape, stick the gingham ribbon around the drum. Attach the ric-rac ribbon around the dome. Wind the satin ribbon through a hole at the top and make 10 strips of ribbon over the dome. Top with a white sugarpaste ball.

Re-roll the reserved white and darker lilac sugarpaste to 2mm thick. With a knife cut into 2cm wide strips, then cut at an angle to form diamonds. I made 16 lilac and 16 white. Allow all decorations to dry out for an hour or two. Attach the white and lilac diamonds around the cake with royal icing and place four sugar pearls between each.

✶ ALSO TRY WITH All-in-one Chocolate Cake (see page 77), or Madeira Cake (see page 99)

TO DECORATE

2kg white sugarpaste
lilac food colour paste
icing sugar, to dust
8 small silver dragees
60g bag white royal icing,
    no. 1 nozzle
1 stick of rock (or 1 extra
    dowelling rod)
1 pot pearlised sugar pearls

SPECIAL EQUIPMENT
20cm round cake board
30cm round cake drum
1.5cm star cutter
6cm horse template
    (see opposite) or cutter
8x30cm white dowelling rods
double-sided sticky tape
24cm circle of stiff white card

FOR THE RIBBONS
Use ribbons of your choice; this
    is what I used:
480cm 3mm-wide ribbon for
    poles, plus 12cm per bow
    (I used 8 different colours)
1 metre 1.5cm-wide purple
    gingham ribbon, for the drum
1 metre 1cm-wide ric-rac ribbon
2.5 metres 1.5cm-wide lilac satin
    ribbon

Coconut and Chocolate Stripy Cake

SERVES 12

FOR THE CAKE

350g unsalted butter, really soft, diced, plus more for the tins

2 tbsp cocoa powder

350g self-raising flour

2 tsp baking powder

6 eggs, lightly beaten

350g golden caster sugar

2 tsp vanilla extract

90g creamed coconut, grated, or grated fresh coconut

FOR THE COCONUT FROSTING

300g cream cheese

150g icing sugar

45g creamed coconut, grated, or grated fresh coconut

1 tsp vanilla extract

FOR THE BUTTERCREAM

150g 70% cocoa solids chocolate

225g unsalted butter, softened

300g icing sugar, sifted

1 tsp vanilla extract

SPECIAL EQUIPMENT

1 large nylon icing bag, with star nozzle

2 x 20cm cake boards

Coconut and chocolate is a winning combination and here two cakes are cut into strips and reassembled to make striped cakes. One to be decorated, the other for the freezer. Make any two-toned flavour or colour. This is best made on the day.

Preheat the oven to 180°C/fan 170°C/350°F/gas mark 4. Butter two 20cm round sandwich tins and line the bases with baking parchment. Make an 8cm high collar of baking parchment for each tin too. Mix the cocoa powder with 1–2 tbsp boiling water, and set aside to cool. To make this cake, I use my electric mixer with the beater attachment, but use a food processor, or a bowl and hand-held whisk if you prefer.

Sift the flour and baking powder into the bowl, add the butter, eggs, sugar and vanilla. Beat until well blended, taking care not to over-mix. Remove half the batter to another bowl. Gently stir the coconut into one bowl and scrape into one of the tins. Add the cocoa paste to the other, stir and scrape into the other tin. Bake both cakes for 30–40 minutes, or until a skewer emerges clean. Remove from the oven and leave the cakes for a minute or two, then run a knife around each to loosen it from the tin. Turn out on to a couple of wire racks. Remove the papers and leave to cool completely.

Meanwhile, to make the coconut frosting, place the cream cheese in a bowl. Sift over the icing sugar and whisk until well blended. Add the coconut and vanilla and mix well. To make the chocolate buttercream, melt the chocolate in a heatproof bowl over barely simmering water, making sure the bowl does not touch the water. Set aside to cool. Beat the butter until really pale and fluffy, then add the icing sugar and vanilla. Beat for five minutes until light and creamy. Add the chocolate and beat again. Take a few spoonfuls and, with a palette knife, place into the icing bag. Only half-fill the bag, or it will make a mess.

Level the tops of the cakes, turn upside down and place on a work surface. Cut the cakes into 2cm strips; each should make 10 strips. Alternate them so each cake has 10 strips of the two flavours. Transfer to the cake boards. Wrap one and freeze for another day.

Using half the coconut frosting, sandwich together the strips of cake and spread the rest over the top and sides. Rest in the fridge for an hour to firm up. To decorate the cake, place it on to an upturned 15cm cake tin. Pipe chocolate roses of varying sizes, from the inside outwards. Practice first on a small plate and scrape the buttercream back into the bag to re-use; it will come to no harm. Lift gently on to a serving plate.

✱ ALSO TRY WITH All-in-one Chocolate Cake (see page 77), and Victoria Sponge (see page 109)

Toffee Apple Pops

Preheat the oven to 170°C/fan 160°C/340°F/gas mark 3½. Butter a 23cm square cake tin and line the base with baking parchment. In a large bowl, sift together the flour, baking powder and cinnamon and stir in the sugar. Peel, core and finely grate the apples. A lot of excess juice may come from the apples; it is very important to squeeze this out using a tea towel, or you will have a soggy cake! To stop the apple from browning, squeeze over a little lemon juice and combine.

Make a well in the centre of the dry ingredients and mix in the grated apples, eggs, melted butter and milk. Stir until just combined, but do not over-mix. Tip into the tin and bake for 35–40 minutes, or until a skewer emerges clean. Stand the tin on a wire rack for a few minutes, then turn out, remove the papers and cool completely.

To make the buttercream, in an electric mixer or in a bowl using a hand-held whisk, beat the butter until really pale and fluffy. Add the icing sugar and beat for at least five minutes more.

To make the pops, crumble the cake into a large bowl, removing any crusty bits. Mix in enough buttercream to hold the crumbs together. You may not need all the buttercream, but this is the quantity I used. Roll the mixture into about 30 balls. Place the balls on a tray lined with baking parchment and chill for several hours, or overnight.

Meanwhile, make the toffee covering. Place the sugar and 60ml water in a small, scrupulously clean, heavy-based pan over a gentle heat. Ensure all the sugar has dissolved, then increase the heat and bring to a boil. Watch all the time until it turns a beautiful golden caramel colour and thickens. Remove from the heat, stand back and add the cream and vanilla. It will splutter and seize, but keep stirring until you have a smooth shiny caramel. Allow to cool for a minute or two. Place each lollypop stick into the caramel, then insert into each cake and dip into the caramel, covering it completely. Place on a tray and return to the fridge to set. Re-shape the pop if it's cracked slightly. The toffee apple pops will keep in the fridge for a day or so. When ready to serve, roll each in a tray of hundreds and thousands to cover.

✱ ALSO TRY WITH Banoffee Cake (see page 42), or All-in-one Lemon Cake (see page 61), or All-in-one Chocolate Cake (see page 77), or Victoria Sponge (see page 109)

MAKES 30

FOR THE CAKE
100g unsalted butter, melted and cooled, plus more for the tin
300g self-raising flour
1 tsp baking powder
1 tsp ground cinnamon
200g light muscovado sugar
3 dessert apples
squeeze of lemon juice
3 eggs, lightly beaten
100ml whole milk

FOR THE BUTTERCREAM
175g unsalted butter, softened
225g icing sugar, sifted

FOR THE TOFFEE COVERING
160g white caster sugar
200ml double cream
1 tsp vanilla extract

TO DECORATE
30 lollypop sticks
hundreds and thousands

Sure to be an enormous success at any children's (or adult's) party and no need to wait for Bonfire Night! You can use any cake recipe, although here an apple cake is dipped into a soft caramel. Make a day or two ahead and keep in the fridge until ready to serve.

Marmalade Syrup Cake

Marmalade is not just for breakfast; use it to make this deliciously moist cake.

Preheat the oven to 180°C/fan 170°C/350°F/gas mark 4. Butter a 20cm, 7.5cm deep round springform cake tin and line the base with baking parchment.

To make the syrup, place the orange juice and muscovado sugar into a small pan and simmer until reduced to a thickish syrup. Allow to cool while you bake the cake.

Sift together the flour and baking powder and stir in the ground almonds. Cream the butter, sugar and orange zest together until light and fluffy; this may take five minutes. Add the eggs very slowly and then, with a large metal or wooden spoon, fold in the flour and ground almond mixture. Lastly, add the marmalade, mixing until well-combined; do not over-mix.

Pour the batter into the cake tin, level the surface and bake for 40–45 minutes, or until a skewer emerges clean. Immediately the cake is cooked, and leaving it in the tin, prick holes all over the surface with a cocktail stick or fine skewer and drizzle the syrup evenly over the surface. Allow the cake to cool completely in the tin. For the frosting, beat the icing sugar into the cream cheese, and add the marmalade and orange zest.

Remove the cake from the tin, keeping it upright. Remove the papers. Split it in half horizontally, and spread the frosting in the middle. Replace the top half. Gently heat the marmalade for the glaze in a small pan, press through a sieve and brush over the cake. Twist the petals of the physalis up to reveal the fruit, if using, and arrange in the centre, or simply scatter with the toasted, flaked almonds.

SERVES 8

FOR THE CAKE
225g unsalted butter, softened,
    plus more for the tin
200g self-raising flour
1 tsp baking powder
50g ground almonds
200g golden caster sugar
finely grated zest of 1 orange
4 eggs, lightly beaten
6 tbsp orange marmalade, plus
    1–2 tbsp to glaze
1 tbsp toasted, flaked almonds
    (optional)

FOR THE SYRUP
120ml orange juice (about 1 large
    orange)
60g light muscovado sugar

FOR THE CREAM CHEESE
    FROSTING
60g icing sugar, sifted
125g cream cheese, at room
    temperature
1 tbsp orange marmalade
finely grated zest of ½ orange

TO DECORATE
a few physalis (optional)

Glamping
Party

Wigwam

SPICED APPLE CAKE WITH CIDER BUTTERCREAM

Take this cool wigwam cake along to the festival, or chill out in the garden instead. Perfect for any festival goer's celebration. If you want to make this as a 'normal' cake, decrease all quantities by one-third and bake in two 15cm cake tins.

TO BAKE

Preheat the oven to 170°C/fan 160°C/340°F/gas mark 3½. Butter three 15cm, 7.5cm deep, round cake tins and line the bases with baking parchment. If you only have two 15cm round tins, then make the full amount of cake batter, divide by three and leave one-third in a bowl. Bake it as soon as a tin becomes free.

Sift together the flour, baking powder, salt, ginger and cinnamon and set aside. Next, toss the apples and sultanas with the lemon juice and 60g of the caster sugar.

In an electric mixer, or in a large bowl with a hand-held electric whisk, beat together the oil, the remaining caster sugar, the muscovado sugar and eggs until light and thick; this should take three to five minutes on a high speed. On a lower speed, add the flour mixture alternating with the milk and vanilla, beating after each addition until smooth. Do not over-mix. Lastly, gently fold in the apples and sultanas.

Divide the cake batter between the tins and bake the cakes for 50–55 minutes, or until a skewer emerges clean. Let cool in the tins for five minutes, then turn out, remove the papers and cool on a wire rack.

In an electric mixer, beat the butter until really pale and fluffy. Add the icing sugar and beat for a further five minutes. Beat in the cider or Calvados very slowly – only a few drops at a time – to avoid splitting the buttercream.

SERVES 15–20

FOR THE CAKE
unsalted butter, for the tins
420g self-raising flour
3 tsp baking powder
1½ tsp salt
1½ tsp ground ginger
3 tsp ground cinnamon
450g eating apples (prepared
    weight), peeled, cored and
    quite finely diced
120g sultanas
juice of ¾ lemon
270g caster sugar
300ml sunflower oil
120g light muscovado sugar
3 large eggs, lightly beaten
335ml whole milk
1½ tsp vanilla extract

FOR THE CIDER BUTTERCREAM
160g unsalted butter, softened
200g icing sugar
4 tbsp cider, or 1–2 tbsp
    Calvados/apple brandy

continued...

TO DECORATE
300g black sugarpaste
icing sugar, to dust
1kg white sugarpaste
red food colour paste
caramel-ivory food colour paste
egg yellow food colour paste
edible glue
Matchmaker chocolates (5 for
    the Wigwam and 2 for the fire)
bunting made from a strip of
    3mm black ribbon and tiny
    triangles of paper (why not
    write your own message?)

SPECIAL EQUIPMENT
20cm round cake board
'V' cutter, or other shape of
    your choice
7cm circle cutter

TO DECORATE

Place a cake on the round board, sticking it on with buttercream. Layer the three cakes with half the buttercream and place one on top of the other. Chill for an hour to make it easier to cut. Stick a skewer through the centre of the cake, right down to the board, and use it as a guide while you cut the cake into a cone shape. When you are happy with the shape, spread the remaining buttercream all over the cake.

Make the doorway by rolling out the black sugarpaste on a work surface dusted with icing sugar to a 6mm thick triangle, measuring 15x15x13cm. Place at the base of the cake. Re-roll the clean offcuts and cut out 20 black 'V's (about 2mm thick).

Take about 50g of the white sugarpaste and roll it out 2mm thick. Cut 18 white circles (I used the end of a piping nozzle). Colour another 100g of the sugarpaste red (see page 168). Colour the remaining sugarpaste using the caramel-ivory and a touch of the egg yellow to make a warm taupe. Make a small cone of 30g taupe sugarpaste to form the top of the wigwam. Next, roll out the taupe sugarpaste to cover the wigwam. It is easiest to do this by dividing it into two; dust the work surface with icing sugar and roll out half the sugarpaste to 6–7mm thick and 25x22cm. Starting by the doorway, fold the sugarpaste around the cake, smoothing with your hands and easing to the edge of the board, as you need to cover it completely. Don't worry if the edge is slightly rough as you can place a strip of red icing over it later on. Cut the sugarpaste to shape and re-use any clean offcuts.

Roll out a second rectangle, again starting at the doorway, and ease around, pressing gently on to the cake, cutting off the excess and joining the sugarpaste at the back.

Make two strips of red icing, both about 2.5x25cm, and attach to the base of the wigwam using edible glue. Make another red band the same width and attach it to the top. Cut out four red circles the same size as the white circles. Finish by rolling the taupe sugarpaste 5mm thick and cutting out a 7cm circle. Attach four red circles. Stick to the top of the wigwam. Attach the white circles and black 'V's on to the cake and stick five Matchmakers into the top. Break the other two Matchmakers to form a little fire. Drape over the bunting.

✶ ALSO TRY WITH All-in-one Chocolate Cake (see page 77), or Madeira Cake (see page 99)

Daisy Chain
ALMOND LEMON BISCUITS

Preheat the oven to 170°C/fan 160°C/340°F/gas mark 3½.

Place the butter, sugar, flour, almonds and lemon zest into a food processor and blitz, stopping once it is combined; do not over-mix. Wrap the dough in cling film and chill for 30 minutes.

Roll out the dough to 5mm thick and cut out the flowers. Make small holes in the centres with a chopstick, wide enough for the lace or ribbon to go through. Chill for 15–30 minutes. Bake for 12–15 minutes. As soon as the biscuits come from the oven, re-cut the holes in the centres. Cool on the trays, then move on to a rack. Once cold, pipe on detail and allow to dry before stringing on to the laces.

✷ ALSO TRY WITH Vanilla Shortbread (see page 186)

MAKES 36

FOR THE BISCUITS
220g unsalted butter, softened
100g icing sugar, sifted
200g plain flour, sifted, plus
    more to dust
100g ground almonds
finely grated zest of 2 lemons
flower cutters (5, 6 and 6.5cm)

TO DECORATE
60g bag white royal icing,
    no. 1 nozzle
lengths of lace sweets or ribbon

Guitar Biscuits
ALMOND LEMON BISCUITS

Make the biscuit dough as above, rest it in the fridge, and roll out to 5mm thick. Using the guitar template, cut out the biscuits. Re-roll and cut more until you have 18. Lay on to baking trays lined with baking parchment and chill for 15–30 minutes. Bake as above for 12–15 minutes. These are fragile and break easily, so cool completely before handling. Colour 30g of the sugarpaste with the claret and the rest a taupe colour (see page 168), using the egg yellow and caramel-ivory.

Dust a work surface with icing sugar and roll out the red sugarpaste to 2mm thick. Cut out 18 stars. Clean and dry the work surface and roll out some taupe sugarpaste to 2mm thick and press on the wood grain mat, if using. Using the guitar template (the biscuits will be slightly larger as the mixture will have spread slightly) cut out guitar shapes, keeping the wood grain in the length of the guitar. Brush with edible glue and attach to the biscuits. Stick on a liquorice sweet, liquorice strings and a star. Pipe a few black details top and bottom. Sprinkle with a little edible glitter. Ready to play!

✷ ALSO TRY WITH Chocolate Shortbread (see page 27)

MAKES 18

1 x Daisy Chain biscuit dough
14cm cardboard guitar template
250g white sugarpaste
claret food colour paste
egg yellow food colour paste
caramel-ivory food colour paste
icing sugar, to dust
1cm star cutter
wood grain-textured mat
    (optional)
edible glue
18 liquorice sweets (or similar)
18 x 12cm strips of liquorice
60g black royal icing,
    no. 1 nozzle
edible clear glitter

Brownies

MAKES 9

150g unsalted butter, diced, plus
  more for the tin
150g 70% cocoa solids chocolate,
  finely chopped
100g self-raising flour
1 tsp baking powder
2 tbsp cocoa powder, plus more
  to dust
260g light muscovado sugar
3 eggs, lightly beaten
1 tsp vanilla extract
100g white (or milk) chocolate
  chips

Remember brownies are different to other cakes: they will still look undercooked when you take them from the oven, because they need to be squidgy!

Preheat the oven to 160°C/fan 150°C/325°F/gas mark 3. Butter a 20cm loose-bottomed square cake tin and line the base with baking parchment.

Melt the butter and chocolate in a heatproof bowl set over barely simmering water, making sure the bowl does not touch the water. Leave to cool a little.

Sift the flour, baking powder and cocoa into a large bowl, then add the sugar, breaking up any lumps. Add the eggs and vanilla. Pour in the cooled chocolate and butter and finally fold in the chocolate chips.

Bake for 45–50 minutes, or until the cake is firmer but still gooey in the middle. The brownies will continue to firm up as they cool. Leave in the tin on a wire rack. When completely cold, cut into brownies, and dust each generously with cocoa powder.

Tiramisu Cake

Preheat the oven to 180°C/fan 170°C/350°F/gas mark 4. Butter two 20cm round sandwich tins and line the bases with baking parchment.

You can use an electric mixer with a beater attachment, a food processor, or a bowl and an electric whisk. First, sift the flour and baking powder into the bowl, add the butter, sugar, eggs and coffee. Beat together until well blended but be very careful not to over-mix, as you want a light cake. Divide the batter evenly between the tins and level the tops.

Bake for about 25 minutes, or until a skewer emerges clean. Remove from the oven and leave for a couple of minutes. Run a knife around the rims to loosen the cakes from the tins and turn out on to a wire rack. Remove the papers and leave to cool completely.

To make the filling, tip the mascarpone into a bowl and lightly beat. Fold in the double cream, sugar and vanilla. Chill until you are ready to assemble the cake.

Split the two cakes in half horizontally, to make four layers. In a little bowl, mix together the coffee and Tia Maria. Assemble the mascarpone filling, the cocoa powder and coffee/liqueur mixture.

To assemble the cake, place one layer of cake on a plate. Sprinkle the coffee/Tia Maria mixture over all four cakes.

Take about a quarter of the mascarpone filling and spread it over the base cake, dust with cocoa powder and place the second tier on top. Repeat until you have a four-tiered cake, topped with the mascarpone filling. Sprinkle the grated chocolate over the top and decorate with the chocolate-covered coffee beans. Chill for an hour or two until ready to serve.

SERVES 10

FOR THE CAKE
225g unsalted butter, really soft, diced, plus more for the tins
225g self-raising flour
1 tsp baking powder
225g golden caster sugar
4 eggs, lightly beaten
2 tbsp very strong black coffee (espresso or instant), cooled

FOR THE TIRAMISU FILLING
250g mascarpone
200ml double cream, very lightly whipped
50g light muscovado sugar
1 tsp vanilla extract
3 tbsp very strong black coffee (espresso or instant), cooled
3 tbsp Tia Maria, dark rum or Kahlua
2 tbsp cocoa powder
30g 70% cocoa solids chocolate, finely grated
15–20 chocolate-covered coffee beans

Tiramisu means 'pick-me-up' in Italian. I have taken the idea of sponge, liqueur, mascarpone, coffee and cocoa beans and created a delicious, rich (strictly for adults) cake perfect for a birthday celebration. Make the cake and filling ahead (even the day before), assembling the cake a couple of hours before it is served. Please make sure you use very strong coffee for this recipe; brew it twice as strong as usual.

Glazed Chocolate-Orange Cubes

FLOURLESS ORANGE SACHERTORTE

FOR THE CAKE

1 x Sachertorte recipe (see page 70), either made with the finely grated zest of 3 large oranges added, or with 55–70% cocoa solids orange-flavoured chocolate (such as Green & Black's Maya Gold), rather than plain chocolate

FOR THE GLAZE

180g 70% cocoa solids chocolate, or 55–70% cocoa solids orange-flavoured chocolate (such as Green & Black's Maya Gold)
100g unsalted butter, cubed
2 tbsp liquid glucose
finely grated zest of 3 large oranges

That famous chocolate orange in a box started life almost a century ago as an apple! Thank goodness it was changed to an orange; a much better combination. Do use orange chocolate in the cake, if you want; it works well here, though I prefer the orange zest. The cake is so moist that it keeps well for a few days and freezes brilliantly. Just make a batch, cut into cubes and drizzle with chocolate as you need. You can buy liquid glucose in the baking department of supermarkets.

When the cake is cold, place it in the fridge for one hour to firm up. Remove from the fridge, turn it upside down and cut into 25 (5x5cm) neat squares. Place on a wire rack, with a sheet of baking parchment underneath to catch the drips.

Melt the chocolate for the glaze in a small heatproof bowl set over gently simmering water, making sure the bowl does not touch the water. Once the chocolate has melted, stir in the butter and liquid glucose until you have a beautiful shiny chocolate glaze. Allow it to cool slightly, then stir in the orange zest. Spread it over the squares with a palette knife and encourage it to drizzle down the sides. Allow to set for half an hour or so and decorate as you wish.

FOR THE DECORATION ... A FEW IDEAS
candles
1 sheet gold leaf or small pot of gold leaf pieces
curls of orange zest
tiny gold dragees
chocolate leaves
milk chocolate curls
Caramel Hazelnut Wisps (see page 173)

Liquorice Toffee Cupcakes

MAKES 12

FOR THE CAKES
12 cupcake cases
1 x Liquorice Toffee Cake batter
  (see page 134)

FOR THE BUTTERCREAM
170g unsalted butter, softened
200g icing sugar, sifted

FOR THE LIQUORICE CARAMEL
100g demerara sugar
60ml double cream
1 tbsp black treacle
30g liquorice (I used two
  6.5cm lengths of soft, sweet
  Australian liquorice), roughly
  chopped

TO DECORATE
piping bag and star nozzle
  (optional)
liquorice allsorts

These are for liquorice lovers only. They are essentially sticky toffee cakes with liquorice and a delicious liquorice toffee buttercream.

Preheat the oven to 180°C/fan 170°C/350°F/gas mark 4. Place the paper cases in a cupcake tray. Divide the batter between the cases and bake for 15–20 minutes, or until the tops spring back to the touch. Remove from the oven, leave in the tins a couple of minutes, then cool on a wire rack.

Make the buttercream by creaming the butter and icing sugar for at least five minutes in an electric mixer (or with a hand-held mixer).

To make the caramel, in a small heavy-based pan, dissolve the sugar with 3 tbsp water over a gentle heat, then increase to a boil. Leave the pan undisturbed for a few minutes, until it turns a lovely rich, caramel colour and has thickened. Give it your full attention at this stage! Remove from the heat and add the cream and treacle, protecting your hands with a tea towel. Stir well, then return to the heat with the liquorice, and bring to a boil. Reduce the heat to very low, stirring all the time, and continue to cook until the mixture thickens.

Remove and leave for all the flavours to mingle and allow the mixture to cool. Taste; it should have a toffee liquorice flavour. Remove the liquorice and, when the caramel is only barely warm, whisk well into the buttercream. (If the caramel is too cold, it will need to be warmed very slightly so it will combine easily into the buttercream. Too hot, and it will melt the buttercream.) Divide the buttercream between the cakes, piping it on if you wish, and decorate with liquorice allsorts.

A
Gardener's
Delight

Vegetable Plot
SPICED APPLE CAKE

SERVES 15–20

TO BAKE

Preheat the oven to 160°C/fan 150°C/325°F/gas mark 3. Butter a 25cm square cake tin and line the base with baking parchment. Pour the cake batter into the tin and bake for 40–45 minutes, or until a skewer emerges clean. Leave to cool completely.

To make the vanilla buttercream, beat the butter until very light and fluffy, then add the icing sugar and vanilla extract and beat for at least five minutes until very light and fluffy.

TO DECORATE

Trim the top of the cake flat. Place the cake upside down on the cake board, adhering with buttercream, then spread the remaining buttercream all over the top and sides. Trim the Matchmakers to slightly different lengths, and press around the sides for the fence.

Colour sugarpaste for the vegetables (see page 168). The amounts and colours listed overleaf are those I used, but feel free to experiment. Keep the coloured sugarpaste sealed in polythene bags, as it will dry quite quickly.

For the potatoes, roll the light brown sugarpaste into a sausage about 1cm thick and cut up into 1–2cm lengths. Roll into uneven shapes and, with the fine end of a paint brush, make indents all over. To make the carrots, take small balls of the orange colour, roll into an elongated cone and press a small knife across it to look like the ridges on a carrot. To make the fronds, roll out a small quantity of the paler green to about 1mm thick. On a work surface dusted with icing sugar, cut small strips about 2cmx5mm. Cut fine lines down one side. Stick on to the ends of the carrots with edible glue.

For the peas, make 3cm-long boat shapes with the paler green, making a point at each end. Indent the centre of each pod with the end of a paint brush. To make the peas, roll tiny little balls of the same colour. Paint the inside of each pod with edible glue and place three peas inside each. To make the cauliflowers, take balls of white about twice the size of a potato and press one side against a sieve to make the pattern. To make the green leaves, press five small pieces of the dark green in your fingers, mark the veins with a knife and glue around the white centre.

FOR THE CAKE
unsalted butter, for the tin
1 x Spiced Apple Cake batter
   (see page 149)

FOR THE VANILLA BUTTERCREAM
200g unsalted butter, softened
300g icing sugar, sifted
1 tsp vanilla extract

SPECIAL EQUIPMENT
25cm square cake board
1cm calyx cutter (optional)

TO DECORATE
2 boxes Matchmakers
icing sugar, to dust
edible glue
edible glaze spray (optional)
few pieces of spaghetti
short piece of green cotton
500g ready-made teddy
   bear-brown sugarpaste
2 tubs chocolate vermicelli

A perfectly ordered miniature vegetable garden, sprouting an abundance of vegetables in neat rows. Each year I try, but mine has never looked anything like this to date… This is an ideal cake for a keen (or like me, aspiring) gardener. All the vegetables can be made weeks ahead and arranged on the cake on the day.

continued...

FOR THE VEGETABLES

FOR POTATOES AND PUMPKIN
STALKS
25g sugarpaste
brown food colour paste

FOR PUMPKINS AND CARROTS
75g sugarpaste
peach/orange food colour paste

FOR PEAS, CARROT AND TOMATO
TOPS, AND BEANS
75g sugarpaste
mint green food colour paste
grape violet food colour paste

FOR LEEK TOPS AND CAULIS
35g sugarpaste

FOR AUBERGINE AND RHUBARB
TOPS AND CAULI LEAVES
50g sugarpaste
mint green food colour paste
Christmas green food colour
paste

FOR TOMATOES
25g sugarpaste
Christmas red food colour paste

FOR RHUBARB STICKS AND
RADISHES
25g sugarpaste
claret food colour paste

FOR AUBERGINES
25g sugarpaste
grape violet food colour paste

For the tomatoes, roll small balls of red, indent the sides slightly with the end of a paint brush and indent a small hole in the top of each. To make the calyx, roll out a small quantity of the lighter green, mould with your fingers and stick on to the top of each tomato (or use the calyx cutter). To make the radishes, simply roll small balls of pink and make one end into a slight point to form the root.

To make the aubergines, roll pieces of purple sugarpaste (about twice the size of a potato) into a ball, then into an oval, slightly narrower at one end. Spray with the edible glaze, if you like. Once they have dried, roll out a strip of the darker green sugarpaste to 1mm thick and cut strips of about 3x1.5cm. Cut zigzags along one side, wrap around the thinnest end of the aubergine and mould a thin stalk.

For the leeks, roll thin sausages of sugarpaste of both the white and brighter green (mine were 2cm white and 2cm green) and join the ends together with your fingers. Cut the green part at an angle and mark lines along the length of each leek with a craft knife. To make the pumpkins, roll a ball of orange about the same size as the aubergine, squash slightly and, with the fine end of a paint brush, mark indents from top to bottom. Make a small hole in the top, roll a stem with a tiny amount of brown sugarpaste and glue into paste.

To make bean canes, cut 8cm lengths of raw spaghetti. Press in twos into the cake in a row and tie the tops together with a piece of cotton to resemble string. Roll thin sausages of the lighter green sugarpaste and twist around the spaghetti. To make the beans, mould very small pieces of the darker green and adhere to the spaghetti with glue. For the rhubarb, roll thin 2cm and 3cm long pieces of pink sugarpaste. Line with a craft knife and mould a leaf from darker green sugarpaste.

For the snail, roll a piece of brown sugarpaste into a very thin sausage and coil around. To make the raised beds, roll out the teddy-bear brown sugarpaste to 5mm thick on a board lightly dusted with icing sugar. Cut out six rectangles, each 10x6cm. Using the glue, arrange all the vegetables in neat little rows on the raised beds. Add the snail. When you are ready to assemble the cake, place the raised beds on top and sprinkle the vermicelli between them. Use a dry paint brush to remove any vermicelli that falls among the vegetables.

★ ALSO TRY WITH Elderflower and Lemon Cake (see page 38)

★ ALSO TRY WITH Elderflower and Lemon Cake (see page 38)

Wellies, Fork and Trowel Biscuits

VANILLA SHORTBREAD

No vegetable plot would be complete without a fork and trowel set and a few pairs of wellies!

Line two or three baking trays with baking parchment. Preheat the oven to 170°C/fan 160°C/340°F/gas mark 3½.

Divide the dough in half. On a lightly floured board, roll out one piece to about 5mm thick. If it is too soft, place the board in the refrigerator if possible to firm up. It will be far easier to cut. Using the wellie template, cut out the biscuits, as closely as you can. Place on a baking tray as you cut them, and re-roll the excess until all the dough has been used. Roll out the other half in exactly the same way and, using the fork and trowel templates, cut out an equal number of each; you should have about 20 of each, after the excess dough is rolled out too. Place in the refrigerator or a cool place to rest for about 30 minutes before baking. To bake, place the trays in the oven for 10–15 minutes.

Colour half the sugarpaste a wellie green, and the other half a red with the red and claret for the garden tool handles (see page 168).

On a clean work surface lightly dusted with icing sugar, roll out the green sugarpaste to about 2mm thick and cut out using the wellie template. Paint a few of the biscuits with the edible glue (or use royal icing) and place a green sugarpaste wellie on to each biscuit. With a small sharp craft knife, score in the detail (or allow the icing to dry for a few hours first and use the black pen). Re-roll the leftover pieces until you have covered all the wellies.

Next, paint the tool part of both the fork and the trowel with liquid silver colour (as it dries fairly quickly paint only two or three at a time). Tip the glitter on to a plate or small tray and dip in the biscuit. With a dry paintbrush, remove any excess glitter. Roll out small sausage-shaped pieces of red sugarpaste to form the tool handles. Using the edible glue, paint the handle end of the forks and trowels and attach red handles. To finish, press in the end of the paint brush or similar tool to form a small hole at the end.

✶ ALSO TRY WITH Chocolate Shortbread (see page 27)

MAKES 20 FORK AND TROWEL SETS
(40 BISCUITS)
10 PAIRS OF WELLIES (20 BISCUITS)

1 x Vanilla Shortbread dough
(see page 186)
plain flour, to dust
wellie, fork and trowel templates
400g white sugarpaste
Christmas green food colour
paste
Christmas red food colour paste
claret food colour paste
icing sugar, to dust
2 paint brushes
edible glue (optional)
60g bag white royal icing
(optional)
sharp craft knife (optional)
black edible pen (optional)
edible liquid silver colour and
rejuvenator
edible clear glitter

Mini Flower Pots
ELDERFLOWER AND LEMON CAKE

MAKES 40 TINY CAKES, AND
18 FAIRY CAKES

FOR THE CAKES
18 fairy cake dark brown paper
  cases and 40 mini muffin dark
  brown paper cases
225g self-raising flour
1 tsp baking powder
225g unsalted butter, really soft
4 eggs, lightly beaten
finely grated zest of 1 unwaxed
  lemon
225g golden caster sugar
2 tbsp elderflower cordial

FOR THE BUTTERCREAM
200g unsalted butter, softened
finely grated zest of 2 unwaxed
  lemons
300g icing sugar, sifted
2 tbsp elderflower cordial

TO DECORATE
100g white sugarpaste
selection of food colour pastes
icing sugar, to dust
selection of flower, leaf and
  butterfly cutters
60g bag of white royal icing,
  no. 1 nozzle (optional)
nylon piping bag and medium
  star nozzle
selection of bought sugar flowers
selection of small edible flowers
  and leaves, such as primulas
  and primroses, violets, violas
  and pansies, sprigs of mint
pearlised sugar pearls
strands of raffia or ribbon

Pack these charming little elderflower and lemon cakes
into a seedling box or a trough as a gift for a gardener.

TO COLOUR SUGARPASTE
Place a piece of sugarpaste on a work surface. Dip a cocktail stick into
a pot of food colour and knead in. It is much better to add the colour
little by little and mix different colours. If it is sticky, add a little icing
sugar. Knead until the sugarpaste is an even colour you like. Seal in a
polythene bag and leave overnight, if possible, to firm up.

TO BAKE AND DECORATE
Dust a work surface and rolling pin with icing sugar. Roll out the
coloured sugarpaste to 2–3mm thick. Using a cutter, cut out shapes
as close together as you can. Re-roll the pieces and repeat. Dry on
a baking tray lined with baking parchment. (Pipe details with royal
icing, if you like.) These keep for months, in dry conditions in a
cardboard box; not in an airtight container.

Preheat the oven to 180°C/fan 170°C/350°F/gas mark 4. Place the
fairy cake cases into two fairy cake tins, and the 40 tiny ones into a
couple of small-hole baking trays. You may need to bake in batches.
For this cake, I use an electric mixer and beater attachment, but use
a food processor, or a bowl and electric whisk, if you prefer. Sift the
flour and baking powder into the bowl, add the butter (in knobs),
eggs, lemon zest and sugar, adding the cordial towards the end. Beat
until well blended; be careful not to over-mix. Divide between the
cases and bake until the cakes spring back to the touch. The tiny cakes
take 10–12 minutes and the larger 12–15 minutes. Remove from the
oven, leave in the tins for a minute or two, then cool on a wire rack.

For the buttercream, beat the butter until really pale in an electric
mixer, or with a hand-held electric whisk. Add the zest and icing
sugar and beat for five minutes until fluffy. Add the cordial slowly,
tasting as you do so; you may not need it all. Put the buttercream into
the piping bag with star nozzle, and swirl on each cake.

I like my flowerpots bursting with blooms so don't hold back! Lay all
your decorations – sugarpaste and fresh – in front of you. Stick them
on to the cakes. Tie raffia or ribbon around each paper case to finish.

✱ ALSO TRY WITH Hidden Fruit and Veg Cakes (see page 94)

Butterscotch Cake

SERVES 8

FOR THE CAKE
175g unsalted butter, really soft, diced, plus more for the tins
175g self-raising flour, sifted
1 tsp baking powder
3 eggs, lightly beaten
100g golden caster sugar
75g light muscovado sugar
1 tsp vanilla extract

FOR THE MASCARPONE
  BUTTERSCOTCH FROSTING
500g mascarpone
1 tbsp black treacle
1 tbsp golden syrup
2 tbsp light muscovado sugar

I love this cake with the not-too-sweet mascarpone butterscotch filling but, if it's for a younger audience or to be made into a sugarpaste-covered cake, you will need to use Toffee Buttercream (see page 42). The reason is, once filled with mascarpone, the cake needs to be kept chilled, which you won't be able to do with a cake covered with sugarpaste. Decorate with the Caramel Hazelnut Wisps (see page 173) at the last minute.

Preheat the oven to 180°C/fan 170°C/350°F/gas mark 4. Butter two 20cm round sandwich tins and line the bases with baking parchment.

I use an electric mixer with beater attachment, but use a food processor, or a bowl and an electric whisk, if you prefer. Sift the flour and baking powder into a bowl, add the butter, eggs, two sugars and vanilla and beat until well blended. Do not over-mix.

Divide the batter between the tins, level the tops and bake for 20–25 minutes until a skewer emerges clean. Remove from the oven, leave in the tins for a couple of minutes, then turn out on to a wire rack. Remove the papers and leave to cool completely.

Meanwhile, make the butterscotch frosting. Tip the mascarpone into a bowl and beat in the treacle, syrup and sugar. Spread a layer on top of both cakes and sandwich them together.

continued...

CARAMEL HAZELNUT WISPS
MAKES 20–24

How did you make that cake? These give instant drama and glamour. Once you have mastered the caramel they aren't difficult. I found inserting the skewer into the nut more of challenge as they can split, so have extra to hand. They can't be made in advance, so make them on the day.

about 30 hazelnuts, blanched
24 fine, pointed wooden skewers,
110g caster sugar
pastry brush

Make sure you have to hand both a small and a large bowl of cold water, and a heavy kitchen board.

Preheat the oven to 170°C/fan 160°C/340°F/gas mark 3½. Scatter the hazelnuts on to a baking tray and roast for five minutes. Cool completely. Insert the point of a skewer very gently into each nut; you may lose a few. Spread newspaper on to the floor and lay a large sheet of baking parchment on it. Directly above it place the heavy board.

Put the sugar and 100ml cold water into a heavy-based saucepan and, over a low heat, allow all the sugar to dissolve, stirring with a metal spoon. Use a damp pastry brush (make sure it's not nylon) to wipe away any sugar crystals from the side. When you can no longer see any crystals, increase the heat to a high boil. Do not stir. It will turn a beautiful golden amber. Drop a piece into the small bowl of cold water. If it crackles and forms a ball, it is ready. Plunge the pan into the large bowl of water and leave to thicken up for a few minutes.

Take a skewered hazelnut and dip into the caramel. Lift, allowing excess to drip into the pan and, when it forms a thin strand, secure the skewer under the heavy board so the caramel can drip on to the baking parchment on the floor. Repeat with all the hazelnuts. If the caramel hardens, return to a very gentle heat to soften. After five minutes, the caramel wisps will have hardened. Snap the lengths as you wish (mine are 10–12cm long).

Very carefully remove the skewers and place the wisps – if possible – directly on to the cake. If not possible, then temporarily rest upright in piece of sugarpaste or buttercream to stop them from rolling around and breaking and keep in a cool, dry place.

Allergen-Free Chocolate Cake

Those with food allergies and intolerances have to celebrate too! This is egg, dairy and nut-free, but is a really dark, moist, quite fragile chocolate cake for everyone to enjoy. If gluten is a problem, then substitute the flour with rice flour, checking that both the cocoa powder and baking powder are gluten-free as well.

Preheat the oven to 170°C/fan 160°C/340°F/gas mark 3½. Oil two 23cm cake tins and line the bases with baking parchment.

In a large bowl, sift together the flour, cocoa powder, baking powder and salt. Stir in the sugar. In another bowl, measure the oil, 400ml water and vanilla extract, then add to the flour mixture, stirring in the vinegar last of all.

Pour the batter into the prepared tins and bake for 30–35 minutes, or until a skewer emerges clean. Leave for a few minutes in the tins, then run a knife around the rims and turn out on to a wire rack. Remove the papers and leave to cool completely.

Put one cake on a cake stand or serving plate, and top with most of the raspberries. Place the other cake on top, and scatter with the remaining raspberries. Sift over an even layer of icing sugar to serve.

SERVES 12

FOR THE CAKE
140ml sunflower oil, plus more
   for the tins
360g self-raising flour
60g cocoa powder
2 tsp baking powder
1 tsp salt
400g golden caster sugar
2 tsp vanilla extract
4 tsp white wine vinegar
400g raspberries
icing sugar, to dust

Savoury Smoked Salmon 'Cake'

TO BAKE

Preheat the oven to 220°C/fan 210°C/425°F/gas mark 7. Lightly butter a 15cm deep round cake tin. Put the wholemeal flour in a bowl and sift in the plain flour, bicarbonate of soda and salt. Rub in the butter with your fingers, then stir in the treacle and sugar.

Make a well in the mixture and slowly pour in the buttermilk. Mix with the blade of a table knife very, very gently. If the mixture is sticky, add a little flour; if it's dry, add a little milk. Turn on to a floured work surface and knead briefly; if you overdo it, it will be tough.

Mould into a round, place into the prepared tin, cut a cross in the top and bake for 45–50 minutes. If it browns too quickly, cover the top with a piece of foil after 30 minutes. The bread is ready when it sounds hollow if you tap the base. Turn out and cool on a wire rack.

Chill the bread in the fridge or freezer for an hour or so; it will be easier to slice. Trim off the top of the loaf, so it is flat. Slice the remaining loaf horizontally four times, to give five horizontal slices.

TO DECORATE

First, prepare the cucumber. Slice very thinly using a swivel vegetable peeler, place in a sieve and lightly salt. Leave for 20 minutes, then dry with a tea towel; you will be amazed at how much liquid comes out. Keep a few curls back for the top. Cut five small strips of salmon and roll up to form little 'roses'.

Once you have sliced your loaf, turn it upside down; the flat base becomes the top. On the bottom slice, spread a thin layer of butter, a little cream cheese, a layer of sliced cucumber, a sprinkling of dill and a layer of smoked salmon. Season well with freshly ground black pepper and a squeeze of lemon juice. You shouldn't need salt. Continue to make a five-layered sandwich. Spread the remaining cream cheese over the top and sides. Place on the salmon 'roses' and reserved cucumber curls.

Chill for 3–4 hours to set (not overnight or the cream cheese might crack). Remove an hour before serving. To serve, cut with a bread knife and a very gentle, slow sawing action. This is important, or it will collapse!

SERVES 10

FOR THE BREAD
50g unsalted butter, softened, plus more for the tin
250g self-raising wholemeal flour
250g plain flour, plus more to dust
1 tsp bicarbonate of soda
1 tsp salt
1 tbsp black treacle
50g caster sugar
284ml carton of buttermilk
a little whole milk, if needed

TO FILL AND DECORATE
1 cucumber
sea salt
200–250g sliced smoked salmon
80g unsalted butter, really soft
400g cream cheese
handful of finely chopped dill
freshly ground black pepper
squeeze of lemon juice

This is for all those who would prefer a savoury cake. If you have never made bread before, this is the recipe for you; it's far easier than a cake! The smoked salmon filling is simply a suggestion: fill this with anything you like. This works best if you bake the bread the day before, cool, then store wrapped in foil.

All-In-One Apricot and Almond Cake

SERVES 8

FOR THE CAKE

175g unsalted butter, really soft,
    diced, plus more for the tin
150g self-raising flour
1 tsp baking powder
75g ground almonds
3 eggs, lightly beaten
175g golden caster sugar
finely grated zest and juice of
    1 large unwaxed lemon
1 tsp almond extract (optional)
250g ripe apricots, stoned
    and sliced

TO DECORATE

100g golden caster sugar
2 squeezes of lemon juice
4 apricots, halved
3 tbsp apricot jam
icing sugar, to dust

TO BAKE

Preheat the oven to 170°C/fan 160°C/340°F/gas mark 3½. Butter a 20cm round cake tin and line the base with baking parchment.

For this all-in-one recipe I use an electric mixer with a beater attachment, but you could use a food processor, or a bowl and an electric whisk.

First, sift the flour and baking powder into the bowl of the mixer. Beat in all the other ingredients (except the apricots), being careful not to over-mix, for a light cake.

Spoon half the cake batter into the prepared tin, level it and sprinkle the sliced apricots over the cake. Spoon the remaining mixture over the top and level the batter. Bake for 50–60 minutes, or until the centre springs back to the touch. Leave in the tin for a few minutes, then turn out on to a wire rack to cool. Remove the papers.

TO DECORATE

Bring 600ml water and the caster sugar to a simmer and add a squeeze of lemon juice. Add the halved apricots and gently simmer for a few minutes. Remove from the syrup, dry on a piece of kitchen towel and cool. Place on top of the cooled cake.

Warm the apricot jam, then press it through a sieve. Place into a clean pan and add another squeeze of lemon juice. Brush over the apricots. Dust with icing sugar before serving with a jug of cream.

This is a very versatile recipe which you can use throughout the summer, ringing the changes by using seasonal, ripe fruit. Try combining sliced, ripe peaches with blackberries or blueberries or try raspberries, sliced plums, halved cherries or even blackcurrants and finely chopped mint (as long as the total weight of fruit is around 250g).

Bakewell Tart

TO BAKE

Lightly butter a 23cm round, loose-bottomed metal flan tin (not ceramic; it won't cook the pastry properly). To make the pastry, tip the flour, salt and icing sugar into a large bowl or food processor. Rub in the butter using your fingertips, or blitz. Lastly, add the egg yolks gradually until the dough comes together. If it is still too dry, add a very little cold water or, if too wet, a little flour. Try not to overwork the pastry as it will toughen it.

To line the tin, lightly flour a work surface and rolling pin. Roll out the pastry to about 3mm thick. Lift it with the rolling pin, line the tin with the pastry and prick all over with a fork. Trim the edges and press well into the tin. Chill for about 20 minutes. Meanwhile, preheat the oven to 180°C/fan 170°C/350°F/gas mark 4. Line the pastry case with a piece of baking parchment and fill with ceramic baking beans (or raw rice). Cook for about 15 minutes, remove the paper and cook for a further few minutes; the pastry will be pale gold. While the pastry is cooling, make the filling.

Place the butter and sugar into the bowl of an electric mixer and beat until pale and fluffy. Start adding the eggs very slowly, then add the almond and vanilla extracts. Fold in the ground almonds. Spread the jam over the base of the pastry, then spoon the almond mixture over the jam – ensuring it is level – and sprinkle with the flaked almonds. Bake for 25–30 minutes, or until the centre is firm to the touch. Cool.

TO DECORATE

To make the two giant cherries, colour the sugarpaste with the claret and Christmas red food colours (see page 168). Divide in half and roll into two balls. Indent the tops of each with the end of a paint brush or similar tool, and spray with the glaze for a shine. To make the cherry stalks, split the vanilla pod nearly in half, keeping one end intact. If necessary trim the two stalks to neaten them, but add the valuable seeds or trimmings to a jar of vanilla sugar. Place the tip of each into the indent in each cherry, and position into the centre of the cooled tart just before serving.

FOR THE PASTRY
100g unsalted butter, chilled and
    diced, plus more for the tin
200g plain flour, sifted, plus more
    to dust
pinch of salt
40g icing sugar, sifted
2 egg yolks, lightly beaten

FOR THE FILLING
125g unsalted butter, softened
125g golden caster sugar
3 eggs, lightly beaten, at room
    temperature
½ tsp almond extract
1 tsp vanilla extract
125g ground almonds
4 tbsp good-quality cherry,
    raspberry or strawberry jam
25g flaked almonds

TO DECORATE (OPTIONAL)
100g sugarpaste
claret food colour paste
Christmas red food colour paste
edible glaze spray
1 vanilla pod

This has become a classic. Created by accident, I understand, in the 1860s in Bakewell, much mystery surrounds its origins... which, surprisingly to us modern fans, didn't include ground almonds. Make sure all the ingredients for the filling are at room temperature.

Nectar Cake

HONEY CAKE

SERVES 12

TO BAKE

Preheat the oven to 170°C/fan 160°C/340°F/gas mark 3½. Lightly butter two 15cm deep, round cake tins and line the bases with baking parchment. Wrap the outside of the tins with a collar of brown paper (or even newspaper) and tie with string, to protect the cakes. Sift the flour, salt and ginger into a large bowl. Melt the butter, honey, sugar and 2 tbsp water in a pan. Cool slightly. Add the eggs, bananas and honey mixture to the flour and mix until smooth. Divide between the tins and bake for 45–50 minutes, or until a skewer emerges clean.

Cream the butter and icing sugar for at least five minutes in an electric mixer (or with a hand-held mixer), add the honey slowly, and mix. Split each cake horizontally to make four layers. Sandwich the layers together with buttercream. The top of the cake should be a cut side so it is flat. Spread the remaining buttercream over the top and sides.

TO DECORATE

Place the granulated sugar into a bowl. In a small bowl, mix 2 tsp water with a little yellow and even less claret food colour to make a rich amber. Blend with the sugar and spread on a tray to dry. Every few hours, mix it. Store in a dry place; it will keep for weeks. Colour the petal paste with yellow and a tiny amount of claret to make an amber (see page 168). Seal in a polythene bag and rest overnight.

Split a polythene bag and place on a work surface. Take 40g of the paste. Flatten the base on to a work surface and indent to shape a cone on top of a rough ball. Dust the small cake board lightly with icing sugar and place the cone in the centre. Take three pieces of flower paste, mould into balls and lay on one side of the bag. Fold over the other side of the bag and flatten each ball until 4–5cm in diameter, keeping one side thicker. Gently peel back the polythene and, taking one petal at a time, mould it around the cone completely covering the top. Take the second petal and place it centrally over the seam of the first (thinnest part uppermost) and mould it around the cone. Place the third petal opposite. Tweak the petals as you work. Keep making the petals and assembling the rose. The outer petals should be 5–6cm in diameter. To support the petals, use little balls of paste tucked underneath; remove when dry. It will completely set in a day. Gently press the coloured sugar over the cake. Top with the sugar rose.

✷ ALSO TRY WITH All-in-one Lemon Cake (see page 61)

FOR THE CAKE
280g unsalted butter, diced, plus more for the tins
350g self-raising flour, sifted
1 tsp salt
3 tsp ground ginger
340g jar runny floral honey
220g light muscovado sugar
4 eggs, lightly beaten
2 ripe bananas, mashed

FOR THE HONEY BUTTERCREAM
300g unsalted butter, softened
200g icing sugar
3 tbsp runny floral honey, to taste

TO DECORATE
200g granulated sugar
egg yellow food colour paste
claret food colour paste
2 x 200g packets white petal paste (see suppliers, page 188)
15cm diameter thin cake board
icing sugar, to dust

A wonderful moist honey cake topped with a giant sugar rose, waiting to be pollinated! Just as beautiful would be to top the cake with fresh roses. Make both the sugar rose and coloured sugar in advance, even weeks ahead, if you like.

Masala Chai Cake
WITH GINGER FUDGE FROSTING

SERVES 12

FOR THE TEA

350ml whole milk, plus more
 if needed
8 cardamom pods, crushed
3 peppercorns
½ cinnamon stick
2 or 3 slices fresh root ginger,
 chopped
2 strong everyday tea bags

FOR THE CAKE

170g unsalted butter, diced, plus
 more for the tin
20 green cardamom pods
230g golden syrup
230g dark muscovado sugar
280g self-raising flour
2 tsp ground ginger
1 tsp ground cinnamon
pinch of salt
2 eggs, lightly beaten

FOR THE GINGER FUDGE
 FROSTING
150g unsalted butter
150g icing sugar
juice of ½ lemon
1–2 tbsp ginger syrup, from a jar
 of stem ginger
2 pieces of very finely chopped
 stem ginger (optional)
red chillies, to decorate
 (optional)

One of my favourite drinks in the world is strong, sweet masala chai, brewed in every home all over India. Here I have turned it into a delicious cake. First, make your tea. You will need 200ml for the recipe. If you wish to drink a cup of tea while you bake, just double these quantities!

Place the milk in a pan. Add the cardamom pods, peppercorns, cinnamon and ginger. Bring to a boil and simmer gently for 10–15 minutes. Once the milk has reduced by almost half, add the tea bags and stew for another minute or so; it does need to be quite strong for the flavour to come through in the cake. Leave to cool. Strain and add more milk, if necessary, to make the total up to 200ml.

Preheat the oven to 170°C/fan 160°C/340°F/gas mark 3½. Butter a square 20cm cake tin and line the base with baking parchment.

To deseed the cardamom pods, split each pod with the point of a sharp knife, empty the tiny seeds into a mortar and grind to a powder with the pestle. If there are any pieces of husk, sift the powder to remove them.

In a pan, melt the golden syrup, butter and sugar. Cool a little. In a large bowl, sift the flour, ginger, cinnamon, cardamom and salt. Stir in the cooled syrup mixture, the eggs and, lastly, gradually pour in the 200ml of chai. Stir gently until well mixed and pour into the prepared tin. Bake for 50–60 minutes, or until a skewer emerges clean. Rest in the tin for a few minutes, then turn out on to a wire rack. Leave until absolutely cold. Remove the papers.

For the frosting, cream together the butter and icing sugar for up to five minutes until light and fluffy. Very slowly add the lemon juice and ginger syrup. Add the stem ginger, if you like. Spread the frosting all over the top of the cake, and carefully transfer to a serving plate or cake stand. Top with a few red chillies, if you want.

Easiest Ever All-In-One Fruit Cake

SERVES 10-12

100g unsalted butter, diced,
    plus more for the tin
60ml rum or brandy, plus
    2–3 tbsp (optional)
160g dark muscovado sugar
50g sultanas
50g currants
50g raisins
1 tsp mixed spice
2 tsp ground ginger
1 tsp bicarbonate of soda
1 egg, lightly beaten
250g self-raising flour, sifted

I cannot believe how simple this is! It is all made in one saucepan and requires no time or skill at all. It is also quite delicious!

Preheat the oven to 150°C/fan 140°C/300°F/gas mark 2. Lightly butter a 15cm, 7.5cm deep, round cake tin and line with baking parchment. Wrap the outside of the tin with a collar of brown paper (or even newspaper works well) and tie with string.

In a largish saucepan, bring the butter, rum, if using, 160ml water (220ml if not using the alcohol), sugar, fruits, spices and bicarbonate of soda to a boil, stirring constantly. Cool down to blood temperature.

Add the egg, stir well, then fold in the flour.

Pour the batter into the prepared tin and bake for 50–60 minutes, or until a skewer emerges clean. Cool in the tin on a wire rack. When cold, prick all over with a skewer and sprinkle with the extra 2–3 tbsp rum, if using. Allow it to soak in, then remove the papers.

Wrap in baking parchment and foil and store until you wish to use it. This is not a very rich cake so it will only keep for a week or so.

Vanilla Shortbread

MAKES 60-100 BISCUITS,
DEPENDING ON SIZE AND
THICKNESS

300g plain flour, plus more
    to dust
½ tsp salt
100g icing sugar
250g unsalted butter, softened
    and diced
1 tsp vanilla extract

Preheat the oven to 170°C/fan 160°C/340°F/gas mark 3½.

Sift the flour, salt and icing sugar into a bowl. Rub in the butter and vanilla extract with your fingers. Gently bring into a ball, wrap in cling film and rest in the fridge for 30 minutes.

Lightly flour a clean board and a rolling pin and roll out the dough to 3–4mm thick. Put the rolled-out dough in the fridge again for 30 minutes, to make it easier to cut. Cut out biscuits with a small cutter.

Lay the shortbread on two baking trays lined with baking parchment and cook for 12 minutes. Leave to cool on the trays.

Marble Cake

Enough for the Volcano (see page 74). To halve the cake, bake in two 20cm round tins for 20–25 minutes.

Preheat the oven to 150°C/fan 160°C/300°F/gas mark 2. You will need three 20cm round sandwich tins. Butter the tins and line the bases with baking parchment. If you have only two tins, make the cake batter and divide it into three batches, baking the third last.

Mix the cocoa powder with 2–2½ tbsp very hot water and stir to make a paste. Set aside to cool. Sift the flour and baking powder into a bowl, add the butter, eggs, vanilla and sugar. Beat until well blended; do not over-mix. Spoon half the batter into the tins (substitute a bowl for the third tin if you only have two). Fold the cocoa paste into the remaining batter with the chocolate chips, and spoon into the tins. Swirl the two cake mixes together with a fork until rippled, level the tops, then bake for 30–35 minutes, or until a skewer emerges clean. Remove from the oven, leave for a few minutes, then run a knife around the rims. Turn on to wire racks, remove the papers. Let cool.

For the buttercream, melt the chocolate, if using, in a bowl over simmering water; the bowl should not touch the water. Set aside to cool. Beat the butter until really pale and fluffy, then add the icing sugar and vanilla. Beat for five minutes until light and creamy. Add the chocolate or cocoa powder and beat again.

SERVES 20

FOR THE MARBLE CAKE
450g unsalted butter, really soft, diced, plus more for the tins
3 tbsp cocoa powder
450g self-raising flour
2 tsp baking powder
8 eggs, lightly beaten
2 tsp vanilla extract
450g golden caster sugar
50g dark chocolate chips

FOR THE BUTTERCREAM
150g 55% cocoa solids chocolate, or 2 tbsp cocoa powder, sifted
225g unsalted butter, really soft
300g icing sugar, sifted
1 tsp vanilla extract

Toffee Cake

Preheat the oven to 180°C/fan 170°C/350°C/gas mark 4. Butter two 20cm and one 15cm round sandwich tins and line the bases with baking parchment. I use an electric mixer with the beater attachment. Sift the flour and baking powder into a bowl, add the butter, eggs, sugars and vanilla and beat until well blended. Do not over-mix.

Divide between the tins to equal depths. Bake for 20–25 minutes, or until a skewer emerges clean. Remove from the oven, leave for a few minutes, then turn on to a wire rack. Remove the papers. Let cool.

SERVES 15

280g unsalted butter, really soft, diced, plus more for the tins
280g self-raising flour
1½ tsp baking powder
5 eggs, lightly beaten
160g golden caster sugar
120g light muscovado sugar
1 tsp vanilla extract

Suppliers

A PIECE OF CAKE
www.sugaricing.com
01844 213428

Swarowski crystals
BEADS & CRYSTALS
www.beadsandcrystals.co.uk
01926 889966

CAKES, COOKIES & CRAFTS
www.cccshop.co.uk
01524 389684

Fresh violets etc
CORNISH COUNTRY
FLOWERS
www.cornishcountryflowers.
co.uk
01736 753479

Edible gold leaf
GOLD LEAF SUPPLIES
www.goldleafsupplies.co.uk
01656 720566

2-litre spherical mould
JANE ASHER
www.janeasher.com
020 7584 6177

Multi-coloured cherries, goji berries
JULIAN GRAVES
www.juliangraves.com
0844 847 6687

LAKELAND
www.lakeland.co.uk
015394 88100

Silver and gold chocolate buttons
MORTIMER & BENNETT
www.mortimerandbennett.co.uk
020 8995 4145

For tropical scene backdrop, pirate candles and food picks (used as flags, see page 84)
PARTY PIECES
www.partypieces.co.uk
01635 201844

Vintage and modern kitchen accessories, including glass cake stands
RE
www.re-foundobjects.com
01434 634567

SQUIRES KITCHEN
www.squires-shop.com
0845 61 71 810

Organic herbs and spices
STEENBERGS ORGANIC
www.steenbergs.co.uk
01765 640088

Wood grain texture mat (for Pirate Galleon, see page 84, and Guitar Biscuits, see page 151); cobblestone texture mat (for Crocodile Handbag, see page 51)
SUGAR ARTISTRY BY
STEPHEN BENISON
www.sugar-artistry.co.uk;
stephen_benison@hotmail.com
01225 768649

Violet liqueur
THEDRINKSHOP.COM
www.thedrinkshop.com
01843 570571

Ribbons, feathers, artificial butterflies, birds
V V ROULEAUX
www.vvrouleaux.com
020 7224 5179

PUBLISHER'S
ACKNOWLEDGEMENTS
The publisher would like to thank the following for loaning accessories and other items:

Assorted chocolates
(see page 71)
ARTISAN DU CHOCOLAT
www.artisanduchocolat.com
0845 270 6996

Hand-decorated Andalucia 20x20cm tiles in Bodegas
(see page 65)
FIRED EARTH
www.firedearth.com
0845 366 0400

For too many lovely pieces to mention, but especially the beautiful tray, tea cup and plates *(see page 56)*
VINTAGE HEAVEN
www.vintageheaven.co.uk
01277 215968

Index

I've been overwhelmed by lovely comments and emails about *Bake & Decorate* and I hope this, my second book, will give as much pleasure.

Special thanks to Anne Furniss for this amazing opportunity, and to all the team at Quadrille. I've so enjoyed working with Claire Peters again, I love your beautiful design work. To Laura Edwards for making my cakes come alive in your gorgeous images, and Alex Lewis for your sensitive styling. Special thanks to Heather Holden-Brown: you are always there for me, and for your wise words.

Lucy Bannell, my editor. Thank you for having so much patience with me and for all your encouragement. I have so enjoyed working with you once again and for all your improvements that I don't even notice, as it still somehow sounds like me!

Rachel Eardley. You have been with me throughout and I can never thank you enough for all your wonderful ideas and creative input. This book would not be the same without you. Anna Tyler. Thank you for being with me in the kitchen and for all your enthusiasm, especially at those times when mine was waning.

Marina Hill and Jade your daughter. You have both been so generous with your time, helped me in the kitchen, but most especially deciphered my handwriting and typed every word. Special thanks to all the following for your contributions and recipe testing (and anyone I've omitted!): Chris Adams, Brian Baker, Monica Hosie, Aaron Paterson, Sally Raeder, Alice Sherwood, Joan Stephens, Amanda Taylor, Charles Taylor, Joan Tyler... and to Sarah Holden who came to my rescue as the book was coming to an end.

Jade Johnston at the Kitchen Range Cookshop in Market Harborough and David Trumper at Jane Asher for helping me with my endless queries and demands!

A huge thank you to all our team at the bakery past and present, and to our loyal customers. Without you none of this would be possible.

Last but not least to Kishore. Thank you for running and developing our business so amazingly and giving me time to work on this book. Kishore, Hari and Tara: over the months while this book has been taking shape you have tolerated sticky surfaces and cakes on every available space in the kitchen and far beyond. Thank you for your patience, which I know was wearing thin by the end, and I hope you feel it was all worthwhile? At least you will be able to choose a special birthday cake from now on!

EDITORIAL DIRECTOR Anne Furniss
CREATIVE DIRECTOR Helen Lewis
PROJECT EDITOR Lucy Bannell
EDITORIAL ASSISTANT Harriet Webster
DESIGNER Claire Peters
DESIGN ASSISTANT Thomas Smith
PHOTOGRAPHER Laura Edwards
STYLIST Alex Lewis
PRODUCTION DIRECTOR Vincent Smith
PRODUCTION CONTROLLER Aysun Hughes

This edition published in 2018 by Quadrille, an imprint of Hardie Grant Publishing

Quadrille
52-54 Southwark Street
London SE1 1UN
quadrille.com

Cataloguing in Publication Data: a catalogue record for this book is available from the British Library.

Text © Fiona Cairns 2011
Photographs © Laura Edwards 2011
Design and layout © Quadrille 2011

ISBN 978 178713 036 4

Printed in China